*The Music
Library*

The History of
Classical Music

Other books in this series include:

The Music Library

The History of Classical Music

by Stuart A. Kallen

LUCENT BOOKS
A part of Gale, Cengage Learning

GALE
CENGAGE Learning

Detroit • New York • San Francisco • New Haven, Conn • Waterville, Maine • London

On cover: Conductor Mstislav Rostropovich conducts an unusual orchestra comprising only cellos.

© 2003 by Lucent Books, a part of Gale, Cengage Learning

For more information, contact
Lucent Books
27500 Drake Rd.
Farmington Hills, MI 48331-3535
Or you can visit our Internet site at gale.cengage.com

LIBRARY OF CONGRESS CATALOGING-IN-PUBLICATION DATA
Kallen, Stuart A., 1955–

Kallen, Stuart A., 1955–
    The history of classical music / by Stuart A. Kallen.
    v. cm. — (The music library)
Includes bibliographical references and index.
Summary: Discusses the evolution of classical music, including the contributions of various cultures and composers. Brief biographical sketches of significant composers are included.
Contents: Introduction: When all music was classical—Music of medieval times—The musical Renaissance—The Baroque era—The classical period—The romantic era—The modern era.
    ISBN 1-59018-123-9 (hardback : alk. paper)
    1. Music—History and criticism—Juvenile literature. [1. Music—History and criticism.] I. Title. II. Music library (San Diego, Calif.)
    ML3928 .K35 2003
    781.6'8'09—dc21

2002003815

Printed in the United States of America
10 11 12 13 14 12 11 10 09 08

• Contents •

• Foreword •

In the nineteenth century English novelist Charles Kingsley wrote, "Music speaks straight to our hearts and spirits, to the very core and root of our souls. . . . Music soothes us, stirs us up . . . melts us to tears." As Kingsley stated, music is much more than just a pleasant arrangement of sounds. It is the resonance of emotion, a joyful noise, a human endeavor that can soothe the spirit or excite the soul. Musicians can also imitate the expressive palate of the earth, from the violent fury of a hurricane to the gentle flow of a babbling brook.

The word *music* is derived from the fabled Greek muses, the children of Apollo who ruled the realms of inspiration and imagination. Composers have long called upon the muses for help and insight. Music is not merely the result of emotions and pleasurable sensations, however.

Music is a discipline subject to formal study and analysis. It involves the juxtaposition of creative elements such as rhythm, melody, and harmony with intellectual aspects of composition, theory, and instrumentation. Like painters mixing red, blue, and yellow into thousands of colors, musicians blend these various elements to create classical symphonies, jazz improvisations, country ballads, and rock-and-roll tunes.

Throughout centuries of musical history, individual musical elements have been blended and modified in infinite ways. The resulting sounds may convey a whole range of moods, emotions, reactions, and messages. Music, then, is both an expression and reflection of human experience and emotion.

The foundations of modern musical styles were laid down by the first ancient musicians who used wood, rocks, animal skins—and their own bodies—to re-create the sounds of the natural world in which they lived. With their hands, their feet, and their very breath they ignited the passions of listeners and moved them to their feet. The dancing, in turn, had a mesmerizing and hypnotic effect that allowed people to transcend their worldly concerns. Through music they could achieve a level of shared experience that could not be found in other forms of communication. For this reason, music has always been part of religious endeavors, from ancient Egyptian religious ceremonies to modern Christian masses. And it has inspired dance movements from kings and queens spinning the minuet to punk rockers slamming together in a mosh pit.

By examining musical genres ranging from Western classical music to rock and roll, readers will find a new understanding of old music and develop an appreciation for new sounds. Books in Lucent's Music Library focus on the music, the musicians, the instruments, and on music's place in cultural history. The songs and artists examined may be easily found in the CD and sheet music collections of local libraries so that readers may study and enjoy the music covered in the books. Informative sidebars, annotated bibliographies, and complete indexes highlight the text in each volume and provide young readers with many opportunities for further discussion and research.

When All Music Was Classical

Prior to the twentieth century when jazz, blues, country, and rock and roll music entered the scene, almost all music was what we today call "classical music." From the 1700s to the 1900s classical music composed for orchestras or instruments such as violin, piano, flute, trumpet, and even guitar was played everywhere from concert halls to restaurants.

Today the term "classical music" has come to define the style of Western music that began in Europe in the Middle Ages and continues today. It includes symphonies, chamber music, opera, and other serious, artistic music. In its earliest form the term was applied to the Viennese classical school, a group of eighteenth-century composers that includes Joseph Haydn, Wolfgang Amadeus Mozart, and Ludwig van Beethoven. In modern times it might also encompass thirteenth-century Gregorian chants, fifteenth-century Renaissance madrigals, twentieth-century classical-jazz compositions by George Gershwin, or avant-garde electric sound pieces of modern composer Karlheinz Stockhausen.

Elements of Classical Music

Classical music—like all other music—is composed of several elements that help define its character. Since music takes place in time, rhythm is the foundation upon which every song is built. Like the beating of the heart, composers determine the feel of music by alternating the pulse, or rhythm, between fast, slow, and medium. Italian terms used in musical notation denote more than a dozen different tempos, or meters, for a piece, including prestissimo—very fast indeed; allegro—fast, cheerful; moderato—moderate tempo; lento—slow; and grave—gravely, very slow.

Within the changing meter of the rhythm, single notes of various pitches, known as melody, are intertwined. In *The Cambridge Music Guide,* Stanley

Sadie and Alice Latham define melody as a "succession of notes in a musically expressive order [and] to most people's minds, melody is the heart of music; no aspect of musical skill is as much prized as the ability to compose melodies that are shapely, expressive and memorable."[1]

Tone color, or timbre, distinguishes the sound and characteristics that separate one instrument or voice from another. For example, the high-frequency treble of a blaring trumpet or crashing cymbal affects the ear much differently than the low breathy tone of an oboe or lilting color of a string section. Com-posers mix these timbres using the various sounds of strings, woodwinds, brass, percussion, and human voice in the same manner that an artist would use different colors to make a painting. As Robert Sherman and Philip Seldon write in *The Complete Idiot's Guide to Classical Music,* "The combined sound of the many instruments within the symphonic ensemble is known as orchestral color. Sometimes the woodwinds predominate, sometimes the strings do; it's the composer's job to mix and match those separate tones until they produce the desired [sound]."[2]

People commonly associate classical music with such composers as Mozart, Hayden, and Beethoven. However, the twentieth-century classical-jazz works of George Gershwin (pictured) also fall into this category.

When the basic elements of rhythm, melody, and color are woven together in classical music, new sounds are derived. For example, two or more complementary notes sounded at the same time are known as harmony. And as Sherman and Seldon write, "[Harmony] enriches the sound of a melody, accentuates changing rhythmic patterns, and gives classical music its special richness and resonance."[3]

Two or more harmonies played together are known as polyphony (Greek for "many sounds") or counterpoint, meaning point-against-point or note-against-note. (Counterpoint is called contrapuntal music.) While these terms may be confusing, they are demonstrated in their most basic form by a group of people singing "Row, Row, Row Your Boat" in a round—that is, one person begins singing the first line after another person has just finished singing that line. In its most complex form, the instrumental works of eighteenth-century composer Johann Sebastian Bach exhibit a fast-moving, intricate counterpoint that continues to astound listeners to this day.

Music and Emotion

When a composer mixes the various elements of music he or she may create a unique sound. The true art of writing and playing classical music, however, is to evoke strong emotions in the listener. In other words, a composer may have technically arranged rhythm, melody, harmony, and color into an impeccable order, but unless the music evokes joy, sorrow, excitement, serenity, or other human feelings, the audience will not be moved.

To express such emotions, classical composers have often based their work on fables, myths, classical tales, or even paintings. These expressive musical stories may feature idealistic heroes, supernatural experiences, and colossal battles between good and evil. For example, "The Erl King" by Franz Schubert, based on a poem by Johann Wolfgang von Goethe, takes place in a forest where a young boy's soul is stolen from him by an evil spirit. On a happier note,

A scene from a performance of Felix Mendelssohn's opera A Midsummer Night's Dream. *The composer's music captured the whimsy of Shakespeare's famous play.*

Felix Mendelssohn set Shakespeare's *A Midsummer Night's Dream* to musical sounds that invoke flying fairies, magical flowers, and a man who turns into a donkey.

While such stories have universal appeal, in centuries past symphonic music was reserved for the rich and powerful. Kings and queens hired court musicians to write and play music for ceremonies, funerals, parties, and even for eating and bathing. English king Henry VIII employed an eighty-man orchestra that followed him around his palace grounds, while his daughter, Queen Elizabeth, would eat a meal only if it was accompanied by orchestral music.

Throughout the centuries, however, classical music has become everyone's music. With nearly universal appeal, the works of Mozart and Brahms may be heard everywhere from the speakers at a shopping mall to formal concerts in China. Compact discs with some of the finest classical works ever written are on sale at record stores, often for incredibly low prices. Libraries lend such music for free.

While all music in the twenty-first century may not be considered classical, the style has transcended fashion and the centuries to find a permanent place in modern culture. With little effort people may familiarize themselves with the evocative melodies of the masters and touch the universal human emotion that binds the past to the present—and people to one another.

Chapter One

Music of Medieval Times

There is a tie between music and religion that is as old as humanity itself. From the earliest times, music has been associated with religious rituals; and from the first ancient civilizations, composers have based many pieces on religious themes. Advances in music took place within a religious context, overseen by priests and holy men. It is through these developments that music was made available to average citizens.

In ancient times prehistoric tribes made crude flutes and drums from wood, bone, and other natural materials. Music was used to celebrate deities, offer prayer, and cast supernatural spells. As William Mann writes in *James Galway's Music in Time,* "Music, in early times, was a form of magic, inducing trance-like concentration in the listener. It soon became apparent that music had greater powers, and could be used as active propaganda to inspire a whole tribe, perhaps to bravery and war."[4]

Musical instruments were widespread and music developed quite rapidly among the first civilizations in Babylon, Egypt, India, and China around five thousand years ago. This ancient music is believed to have been used mainly for sacred ceremonies and cultural celebrations. While no record of this music has survived, pictures of instruments were widespread in paintings. These show that ancient people played primitive versions of instruments such as harps, drums, and trumpets, found in their updated forms in modern symphony orchestras.

Greek and Roman Music

The origins of modern classical music evolved during the fifth century B.C. in ancient Greece. This era, known as the Greek classical period, saw a flowering of the arts as philosophers, poets, dramatists, and painters created works that are still revered today. Music was most often played to accompany poetry, dance, and dramatic plays, or used to accompany government or religious functions. Musicians at these celebrations played Greek versions of modern instruments such as a harplike lyre, called kithara, and the double-reed aulos, the forerunner of the oboe. It is believed that the music played at this time did not employ harmony and was generally improvised, or made up on the spot, by the musicians.

Greek civilization faded and the powerful Roman Empire took its place. At this time the shrill shriek of trumpets and other brass horns were used to frighten enemies during battle. But music had a more important role to play in the glory days of the Roman Empire in the first two centuries A.D. As in modern times, the Romans used large orchestras and choruses that featured extremely skilled musicians, or virtuosos. And just as European kings and queens supported the musical arts in later centuries, so too did the Roman emperors.

Modeling their compositions on classical Greek music, the Romans intertwined their songs with poems, verses, and words, while improvising musical lines. And music was considered more than just idle entertainment—as a phenomenon of nature, music was believed to be powerful enough to influence the thoughts and behavior of human beings.

The Influence of the Early Church

While the Romans dominated the early years of the first millennia, the Jewish people carried the Old Testament of the Bible through their travels in the Middle East, southern Europe, and elsewhere. Music is well noted in the Bible, from Gabriel blowing his silver horn to Saul being told by Samuel (1 Sam. 10.5), "As you approach the town you will meet a band of seers coming down from the high place with harp, drum, pipe and lyre playing before them while they prophesy."

Such biblical quotes demonstrate that music and human spirituality have long been intertwined. When Emperor Constantine decreed in A.D. 325 that Christianity would become the official religion of the Roman Empire, officials within the Church began to shape and direct the course of music. Donald Jay Grout explains in *A History of Western Music:*

> Certain features of ancient musical life were definitely rejected—for example, the idea of [playing] music purely for enjoyment as an art. Above all, the forms and types of music connected with the great public spectacles such as festivals, competitions . . . [and] dramatic performances . . . were regarded by many as unsuitable for the Church. [5]

Leaders in the Church believed that music should be limited mainly to the singing of psalms, hymns, and prayers. The Church adapted ancient Jewish musical practices; particularly, the manner in which psalms were sung, a technique known as responsorial psalmody. During this type of holy song, a lead vocalist sang the first line of a psalm

Greek Music and the Church

In A History of Western Music *Donald Jay Grout compares classical Greek music with that produced by the Christian church in later centuries.*

Although we do not know much about Greek music or its history, we can say that in three fundamental respects it was the same kind of music as that of the early Church. In the first place, it was primarily monophonic, that is, melody without harmony or counterpoint. . . .

In the second place . . . musical performances . . . were improvised. The performer was, to a certain extent, also the composer. This does not mean that what he did was completely spontaneous and unprepared; he had to keep within the . . . accepted rules governing the . . . styles of music suitable for particular occasions . . . but outside these restrictions he had considerable freedom. He was not playing or singing something he had memorized or learned from a score, and consequently no two performances of the "same" piece were exactly alike. Improvisation . . . [also] prevailed . . . in our Western music up to perhaps the eighth century A.D., and the practice continued to affect musical styles for a long time: even after precise musical notations were invented. . . .

Thirdly, Greek music was almost always associated with words or dancing or both; its melody and rhythm were . . . bound up with the melody and rhythm of poetry, and the music of the religious cults, of the drama, and of the great public contests.

A musician from ancient Greece is pictured on this fifth-century vase, the era from which modern classical music emerged.

alone and the congregation responded by singing the second line in unison.

As the influence of the Christian church spread through the Mediterranean regions of the Middle East, Africa, and Europe, the Church incorporated the musical styles of the people who lived in those areas. In that manner some early hymns were adapted to folk songs and traditional music of specific regions.

The Influence of Pope Gregory

The influx of new psalms and hymns from many lands presented a problem for religious leaders. Secular, or non-religious, music had been adapted into the hymns over the centuries. In A.D. 600 Pope Gregory the Great took on the task of standardizing and codifying church music, purging secular songs from church services. To do so, Gregory designated specific music for various church services throughout the seasons while eliminating music he considered profane or irreligious.

The most important feature of Gregory's work was to make Mass the center of Christian religious services. As a ritual enactment of the Last Supper, masses are held on holidays such as Easter, Christmas, saints' birthdays, funerals (requiem mass), and other events. The text of the Mass was chanted in Latin, and in a High Mass many sections of the words were sung.

Gregory needed a way to simplify the teaching of Mass melodies to church choirs. At this time, individual

Pope Gregory the Great developed the mode, a simple method for teaching Mass melodies to church choirs.

notes did not have letters such as A, B, C, and so on. Gregory devised a simple method, called modes, whereby he gave each note a letter of the alphabet while giving various eight-note scales names from ancient Greece.

By using a piano (an instrument that did not exist in Gregory's day) a listener can play the scale of a Dorian Mode by hitting all the white notes on the piano from D to D, that is, D E F G A B C D. The Lydian Mode consists of the notes from F to F. The Mixolydian Mode consists of notes from G to G (and may be heard in the Beatles' song "Norwegian Wood").

Together the modes were used in the singing of Gregorian chants, also known as plainsong, explained by Dhun H. Sethna in *Classical Music for Everybody:*

Here, the music of the entire Mass consisted of a single, repetitively chanted line, trance-like and deeply mystical, [without] any instrumental accompaniment. . . . Only the unadorned human voice with a single-minded focus of attention [was seen as] worthy enough to become a medium between heaven and earth. Sometimes, soloist and congregation would alternate; sometimes, the congregation was divided to sing alternate verses and then come together. Over time, the chant developed into a very sophisticated form of . . . rhythm. [6]

Each community had its own versions of Gregorian plainsong, and over three thousand such melodies survive today. Every plainsong originally had its own specific purpose during various church ceremonies, and many of these songs formed a basis for Christian religious music throughout the Middle Ages.

The influence of plainsong spread across Europe after Gregory established the *Schola Cantorum,* the first singing school in Rome where singers could learn the plainsong chants. The significance of this work is discussed in *The Story of Music* by Paul Bekker:

Gathering of the entire treasure of ecclesiastical music into a mag-

nificent . . . system, Gregory [established] music as an independent and important part of worship. . . . Schools for singers . . . were now added in Italy and later on in the neighboring countries to the north. . . .

Gregorian plain-song, an achievement of the first rank not only in music but in general culture, is the great contribution of the first ten centuries of Christendom. [7]

Although Gregorian chants fell out of favor in later centuries, in the 1990s they became incredibly popular. The 1994 album *Chant,* by the Benedictine Monks of Santo Domingo de Silos, sold over five million copies within a year. The compositions, which date back to the eleventh century, brought so much attention to the monks that they made formal requests to journalists to leave them alone. When that failed the monks recorded several follow-up albums and went on a world tour. This overwhelming popularity lies in the music, as Grout describes it:

The Gregorian chants are one of the great treasures of Western civilization. . . . [They] stand as a monument to medieval man's religious faith; they were the source and inspiration of a large portion of all Western music up to the sixteenth century. They constitute one of the most ancient bodies of song still in use anywhere, and include some of the noblest artistic works ever created in pure melody. [8]

The invasion of Spain by king Charlemagne (on horseback) was the colorful subject of the lengthy chanson "Song of Roland."

Songs of the Troubadors

Gregorian chants satisfied the needs of religious institutions in the Middle Ages, but secular songs flourished among the educated nobility such as kings, queens, and other rulers. In an age when there were only a few handwritten books, and no newspapers, nobles wanted to hear about patriotic deeds and the heroic actions of revered rulers. For this they turned to the style of French popular music known as chansons de geste, "songs of action," that were played from about 800 to 1100.

These epic chansons contain four thousand to fifteen thousand verses that are essentially musical history lessons. For example, the four thousand lines of the "Song of Roland" detail the invasion of Spain by Frankish king Charlemagne (Charles the Great), whose eighth-century kingdom included almost all of western and central Europe. The first verses of the chanson are taken from the complete epic poem printed on the "The Song of Roland" website:

> Charles the King, our Lord and Sovereign,
> Full seven years hath sojourned in Spain,
> Conquered the land, and won the western main,
> Now no fortress against him doth remain,
> No city walls are left for him to gain,
> Save Sarraguce, that sits on high mountain.
> Marsile its King, who feareth not God's name,
> Mahumet's man, he invokes Apollin's aid,
> Nor wards off ills that shall to him attain. [9]

Such poems were hand copied on small manuscripts that could be carried by wandering minstrels known as troubadours or, depending on the region, gleemen, scops, jongleurs, or goliards. In Germany they were called minnesingers, or "singers about love," an appropriate name because in addition to writing and singing the serious chansons, the minstrels performed short, joyous love songs that celebrate "courtly love." This style of music was popular between 1100 and 1300, and as Sadie and Latham write, the troubadour's "love-lyrics . . . often idolize women as beautiful and unattainable." [10]

Not all songs were about love, however, and the chansons have various names according to their content, and when and where they were to be performed. A courtship song sung in the evening is called a serenade. The *aubade* is a morning song. The *servantes* celebrates the deeds of a prince; the *tenzone* is something of a medieval protest song that heaps scorn upon a well-known person. *Pastourelles* are songs that idealize shepherds and place them in supernatural situations with fairies and wood nymphs. And roundelays repeat the same refrain after every verse.

The First Composers

The troubadours entertained rich and poor alike, singing solo or accompanying themselves with lutes, harps, and violin-like instruments known as the *lire da braccio*. Many of the troubadours were born to nobility and were renowned counts, knights, squires, and princes. Because of their high stations in life, their names were recorded in royal books, and these men—Bernart de Ventadorn, Adam de la Halle, Mar-

The English Bards

Around the tenth century A.D., *English musicians known as bards drew on the music of the ancient British tribes, the Celts. In* A Popular History of Music *W.S.B. Mathews discusses the bards.*

[B]ards] were divided into three great classes. The first class was . . . historians . . . who . . . took up the [songs] of [fortune-tellers] and prophets. The second class was composed of domestic bards . . . [who] were chiefly devoted to [telling the tales] of their wealthy patrons. The third class, the heraldic bards, was the most influential of all. They wrote the national [histories in song]. . . .

The musical bards were divided into three classes. In the first were the players upon the harp; they were called doctors of music. To be admitted into this class it was necessary that they should perform successfully the three . . . most difficult pieces in the bardic repertory. The second class of musical bards was composed of the players upon the [violin-like] crwth, of six strings. The third class were the singers . . . [who were also] true doctors of music.

cabru, Guiraut Riquier, and Thibaut—are the first composers who are remembered by name. Some were even immortalized in opera in later centuries. For example, the twelfth-century minnesinger Walter von der Vogelweide is depicted in Richard Wagner's 1845 epic *Tannhäuser*.

Some troubadours were quite influential as keepers of news, information, and history. Although their simple melodies lack harmony or complexity, the wandering folksingers exerted a positive influence on music that has lasted throughout the ages.

The Rise of Harmony

While troubadours were composing single-note melodies to accompany their poems of love and action, a new style of harmony singing developed within the Church. This was known as organum because voices were accompanied by the organ, an instrument developed around the ninth century and widely found in churches throughout Europe.

The vocal portion of organum consists of three-part harmony, that is three voices singing complementary notes together. One person sings the main melody, the second sings the same notes but an octave (eight notes) above or below the first. Meanwhile, a third person sings in the middle range, above or below the main melody. In later centuries the simple style of organum was embellished so that the different voices sang shorter or longer notes, resulting in a richly varied melody.

The Invention of Do-Re-Mi

As organum grew in popularity, a new method for teaching the complex harmony to church choirs became necessary. To do so, the familiar "do-re-mi" singing method was invented around 1030 by a monk named Guido of Arezzo (Italy), who was a choirmaster in charge of teaching organum and other styles.

In order for his students to learn "by ear" Guido developed names for six notes (C-D-E-F-G-A) based on a popular Latin hymn called *Ut queant laxis*. Guido cleverly used the first two letters of the first words in each line to name the corresponding notes, ut-re-mi-fa-sol-la. (The verses of the song were *UT queant laxis, REsonare fibris, MIra gestorum, FAmuli tuorum, SOLve polluti, LAbii reatum*). The notes are taught the same way today, but *ut* has been replaced by *do,* and *ti* has been added above *la*.

In addition to the do-re-mi system, the monk developed another teaching aid known as the "Guidonian Hand" so choirboys could learn to "sight sing." Guido assigned one of twenty notes to the knuckles and joints of his hand and the tips of his fingers. Students could sing the notes as the monk pointed to the various parts of his left hand with his right index finger. This method of teaching proved to be so helpful that over the centuries a drawing of the Guidonian Hand was included in nearly every musical textbook.

Some have even speculated that each of the five lines of the modern musical staff, upon which musical notation is written, may represent Guido's fingers.

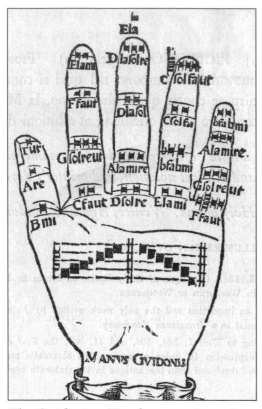

The Guidonian Hand was an ingenious concept used to teach choirboys to sight sing.

Grout writes: "The invention of the staff made it possible to notate precisely the . . . pitch of the notes of a melody, and freed music from its . . . exclusive dependence on oral transmission. It was an event as crucial for the history of Western music as the invention of writing was for the history of language." [11]

Polyphonic Perspective

With the development of harmony and new methods for teaching, music continued to mature. This musical complexity corresponded with other changes taking place in twelfth-century Europe. As the population noticeably increased, many of today's modern cities were founded throughout the continent. This fueled the growth of schools and universities. In the world of art, painters began to experiment with perspective and depth, adding a new dimension to art.

Music, too, was gaining perspective and depth. The days of improvised melodies gave way to the art of writing new compositions. Aided by the newly developed musical notation, original works of music became permanent and available to any player who could read the notes. The universal language of a musical score also allowed a piece to be taught to others no matter where they lived. As Grout writes, "The score . . . was a set of directions which could be executed whether or not the composer was present. Thus composition and performance became separate acts instead of being combined in one person as before, and the performer's function became that of a mediator between composer and audience." [12]

The art of composition also allowed music to take on new characteristics, particularly polyphony, in which two or more different melodies are combined to give the music a richness, strength, and power unheard in Western music until that time.

Two of the first composers of polyphonic music are known as Léonin, who lived in the 1170s, and Pérotin, who lived in the first part of the 1200s. Both men were choirmasters at the

Church of Notre Dame in Paris. Together, their style of music along with compositions by dozens of other unknown composers is referred to as the Notre Dame School.

Léonin's work is known throughout the world today because he wrote the *Magnus liber organi,* or the "Great book of organum," modern versions of which are still in print. Léonin wrote mainly for two voices but his book was later revised by Pérotin, who added three or even four voices to the works. The polyphonic songs of the Notre Dame School, according to Mann, are "soaring, magnificent and [resounding]—and . . . laid the foundation of a polyphonic style whose flowering was to last some 400 years." [13]

Motet

Organum has two distinct parts, and a new type of music, known as motet, evolved from one of these parts. The fixed melody of organum, called "fixity," follows an unchanging part. The other part is called "freedom," or descant, and describes the harmonious singing that weaves, dives, and soars between the fixed melody. When Pérotin composed his polyphonic organums, he would oftentimes write dozens of freedom sections that a choir could sing over a single fixity section. Each freedom part is varied in tempo, key, and musical color and could be used for specific rituals, depending on the mood desired. At first these freedom sections did not have words, but

Early Musical Notation

As more complicated melodies were invented, new ways of writing music became necessary. In James Galway's Music in Time *William Mann describes the new method of musical notation.*

The possibility of a singer [hitting the wrong note] must have hastened the arrival of a more sophisticated musical notation. Sure enough, in about A.D. 871, a monk living . . . in northern France wrote out the Greek and Latin texts . . . [and] drew . . . [many] signs to indicate pitch, duration [of the note] and stress. They are called *neumes* (from a Greek word meaning nod or sign). . . . [During] the tenth century they became commonly used throughout France, Germany and Britain, and developed into staff notation, which was able to give comprehensive and precise directions for musical performance.

This English reproduction of Mozart's motet manuscript demonstrates the composer's first effort at writing choral music.

during the thirteenth century sacred texts—or even secular poems—were added. Eventually these freedom sections were recognized as unique songs separate from the organum from which they originated.

The freed melodies are known as motets, derived from the French word *mot* or "word," because words had been added to the original freedom section. Thousands of motets were written during the thirteenth century and many of those survive today. While their authors remain unknown, many are believed to have been written by composers of the Notre Dame School who succeeded Pérotin.

As the thirteenth century drew to a close, the Church had generated thousands of harmonious and complex compositions, while secular musicians created songs of love and war. Ways had been devised to write music on a page and teach it to ever expanding numbers of people. As more musicians learned the arts of harmony, rhythm, and polyphony a quest for new songs sparked a musical renaissance that permanently changed the nature of song.

Chapter Two

The Musical Renaissance

By the 1300s musical development had been dominated by the Church for nearly five hundred years. While average citizens occasionally listened to wandering troubadours, it was the popes, choirmasters, and other Church officials who oversaw the development of harmony, counterpoint, and additional musical techniques that were to become the basis for classical music.

The Church began to lose its power, however, by the late fourteenth century, a time when long catastrophic wars, the Black Plague, and religious infighting caused many to lose their faith in religion. As people began to call Church doctrine into question, composers, artists, and writers turned to classical Greek culture for spiritual inspiration. This led to a movement in music, art, and literature known as the Renaissance (Italian for "rebirth"), which lasted from approximately 1400 to 1600.

The outburst of creativity during the Renaissance was motivated by an intellectual movement known as humanism, a belief system that emphasizes the personal worth of the individual—and the importance of human values—as opposed to religious dogma. As Sethna writes, "With the Renaissance came a sweeping wave of earthly feeling and expression, and a rebellion against the . . . intellectual domination of the Church."[14] With this new spirit the creative focus of the era was on the secular music that could be understood and performed by the average person even as some composers continued to write religious music.

The New Art

The roots of Renaissance music were planted in the fourteenth century with the *ars nova,* or new art, movement named after an essay by composer Philippe de Vitry, written around 1320 in Paris. (*Ars nova* is used to differentiate the era from what musical historians call *ars antiqua,* or "the old art"—the achievements of the thirteenth century such as chant, polyphony, motet, and so on.)

The music of the *ars nova* composers is more complex than earlier music. While it may not seem revolutionary to modern ears, the style was a distinct break with the past. The music was even condemned by the pope because the *ars nova* sound emphasizes secular concerns such as imagination and creativity, as opposed to religious dogma and belief.

While writing the *ars nova* paper, de Vitry invented a system of time signatures that allowed composers to write new rhythmic patterns into their music. *Ars nova* composers wrote parts for voices that repeat rhythmic patterns of a dozen or so notes over and over. Called isorhythm, this is used as a foundation for songs over which other vocal parts are intertwined. De Vitry used his

A priest ministers to victims of the Black Plague. During this deadly epidemic, people began to lose faith in the Church and artists turned to Greek culture, music, and literature for inspiration.

theories to write dozens of pieces. Perhaps the most revolutionary aspect of his songs, however, was the provocative words that ridiculed the pope and the Church hierarchy.

De Vitry's work was continued by Guillaume de Machaut, a poet, politician, and composer. In the spirit of the new age, Machaut wrote mostly secular music despite the fact that he was in the respected Holy Orders and was made Cannon of Rheims in present-day France. Despite his association with the Church, Machaut often wrote passionate songs of love.

Machaut was so dedicated to secular music that of his 140 pieces that are known today, only seven are liturgical, that is, written for church ceremony. The rest were composed in the popular song styles of the day and are similar to poetry that uses repeated refrains and alternating verses with repetitive sections. These songs are categorized as ballades, *virelais,* rondeaux, *lais,* and motets, and as Sadie and Latham write, "Machaut's music looks both backwards, to the thirteenth century and the age of chivalry, and forwards, to the fifteenth century and the early Renaissance." [15]

The Universal Man

By the middle of the 1400s secular music was growing in importance, and musicians in France, Italy, and England were the most innovative of any in Europe. People in Italy, in particular, were pursuing a new path in the arts by, ironically, studying the distant past for inspiration. Looking beyond the rigid constructs of Church doctrine, Italian intellects unearthed the works of ancient Greek and Roman scholars who spoke of intellectual freedom and the *uomo universale,* "universal man," or the "man whole and complete." [16]

The focus on human feeling and emotion spread throughout society and fueled a renewed interest in secular music which became one of the primary forms of entertainment for all classes of people. In the sixteenth century while traveling in Tuscany, Italy, French philosopher Michel de Montaigne noted this development, writing that he was "astounded to see peasants with lutes in their hands, and, besides them, shepherds reciting [poetry] by heart." [17]

Music was so popular that it was depicted in hundreds of Renaissance paintings, from angels playing harps to beautiful maidens on riverbanks strumming lutes. This trend was also written about in books, as Will Durant writes in *The Renaissance:*

> [Renaissance] literature . . . conveys a picture of a people singing or playing music in their homes, at their work, on the street, in music academies, monasteries, nunneries, churches, in processions . . . and pageants, in religious or secular plays, in the lyric passages and interludes of dramas. . . . Rich men kept a variety of musical instruments in their homes, and arranged private [music programs]. Women organized clubs for the study and performance of music. Italy was . . . mad about music.

The popularity of music during the 1400s inspired many Renaissance artists to adopt it as a theme in their paintings.

Folk song flourished at all times, and . . . popular melodies were adapted for complex madrigals, for hymns, even for passages in music for the Mass. "In Florence," says [sculptor Benvenuto] Cellini, "people were wont to meet on the public streets of a summer night" to sing and dance. Street singers . . . strummed their sad or merry notes on handsome lutes; people gathered to sing *laudes,* hymns of praise, to the Virgin before her street or roadside shrines; and in Venice mating songs rose to the moon from a hundred gondolas, or throaty lovers hopefully serenaded hesitant lasses in the mystic shadows of labyrinthine canals. Almost every Italian could sing, and nearly as many could sing in simple . . . harmony.[18]

Music was important to people of all social classes, and even the wealthy were not considered truly refined unless they knew how to read music and play an instrument. These people were able to improve their talents by attending some of the hundreds of music schools and academies found throughout Italy.

Royalty spent more on music than almost any other art, paying large sums of money to draw talented singers, musicians, and composers to their courts. These leaders also supported a wide array of craftsmen who built precious and valuable harpsichords, organs, lutes, and other instruments.

With so much attention focused on secular music, cathedrals began to dramatically improve their musical offerings. In major cities such as Venice, Milan, and Naples, choirs of nuns drew huge crowds when they sang chants at worship services known as vespers. The churches competed fiercely with one another to attract the best singers, choir

Printing Music Books

In A History of Western Music *Donald Jay Grout describes how the invention of the printing press helped make advances in music.*

One of the most important factors in the growth of music during the Renaissance was the rise of music printing. The art of printing books from movable type, perfected by Johann Gutenberg by 1450, was applied to liturgical books with plainchant notation about 1473. . . . The first collection of polyphonic music printed from movable type was brought out in 1501 by Ottaviano de' Petrucci at Venice. By 1523 Petrucci had published fifty-nine volumes . . . of vocal and instrumental music. His publications, especially the earliest ones, are models of clarity and accuracy. . . .

Most published ensemble music in the sixteenth century was printed in the form of partbooks—one small volume, usually of oblong format, for each voice or part, so that a complete set was requisite for performances. Partbooks were intended primarily for use at home or in social gatherings. Most church choirs continued to use the large handwritten choirbooks; new ones were still being copied in the sixteenth century, although a few publishers also printed large choirbooks. . . .

The application of the art of printing to music was obviously an event of far-reaching consequence. Instead of a few precious manuscripts laboriously copied by hand and liable to all kinds of errors and variants, a plentiful supply of new music was now made possible—not exactly at a low price, but still less costly than equivalent manuscripts, and of uniform accuracy. Furthermore, the existence of printed copies meant that now many more works of music would be preserved for performance and study by later generations.

directors, organ players, and other musicians, who acted as magnets for the masses.

Guillaume Dufay

Ironically, while the Renaissance inspired an incredible array of Italian musicians, painters, and sculptors, there were few Italian composers remembered from that era. Italy was a wealthy country, however, and the flowering of the arts there, combined with the generous financial patronage of the nobility, attracted composers from the north, particularly northeastern France and Flanders (present-day Belgium). One of the most famous musical geniuses of the day was Guillaume Dufay, born around 1400 in present-day France in the Burgundy region, one of the most musically active areas of fifteenth-century Europe.

Dufay spent much of his life traveling Italy, absorbing Renaissance culture, and contributing to the musical language of the era. In his early career he wrote a more traditional style of polyphonic chant used for liturgical purposes. Later he wrote dozens of secular chansons in French concerning love, the beauty of nature, and even the pleasures of wine.

Dufay's music was widely published and performed throughout the cosmopolitan cities of Europe and he composed for popes, dukes, and kings. Combining harmony and unresolved sounds called discord, he permanently changed the sound of music. The motet *Vasilissa,* written for the wedding of a Byzantine prince, is described by Mann as "a moment of ingenuity and splendid composition—the voices blazing forth in celebration." [19] His chansons are described by Charles van den Borren in *Ars Nova and the Renaissance 1300–1540* as "airy or graceful or serious or sad . . . [or] full of life and color . . . [while in others] the emotions of love are expressed with a frank and tender elegance." [20]

Dufay could touch the heart of the listener with celestial music and sentimental words as in the rondeau *"Pour l'amour de ma doulce amye,"* the lyrics of which are translated into English:

> For the love of my sweet mistress
> I would sing this roundelay.
> And with good heart present it to her
> So that she may be more pleased.
>   . . .
>
> She is fair, pleasant and joyful,
> Wise in manner and in speaking:
> I would serve and love her
> To the height of my power all my life. [21]

At other times Dufay could be comic or even crude as he sings about drinking and fighting in the rondeau *"Puisque vous estez campieur"*:

> Since you are a fighter
> Willingly I will fight with you,
> To know if I could
> Be as good a drinker as you. . . .
>
> You think that I am a bad drinker,
> But three cups I would easily drink,
> Truly, or I would pass
> As the worst in the world. [22]

The Age of Dufay

In Ars Nova and the Renaissance 1300–1540, *Charles van den Borren describes the work of Guillaume Dufay, one of the foremost composers of the Renaissance period.*

R enowned for the greatness of his genius, Dufay's name was known to all. Sought after by the [rulers] of the earth, not only in the Church but also in the royal, princely, and baronial courts of the Burgundian [region], of France and of Italy, he moved about from youth to old age with the utmost freedom, riding over hill and dale from one court to another . . . [with] the Pope or the Duke of Savoy. . . .

Thus it came about that he chronicled in song the affairs both great and small of Europe's social and religious life. When barely twenty years old he was called upon to celebrate the wedding of Theodore, son of the Byzantine Emperor Emmanuel Palaeologus. . . . In 1436 he composed [a] delightful motet . . . for the consecration of the Cathedral at Florence, Santa Maria del Fiore. . . . Lastly the motet 'Ave regina coelorum', [was] destined for his own deathbed. . . .

It is therefore not at all surprising that modern historians have described the first sixty years of the fifteenth century as "the age of Dufay". He was the dominating musical personality of the time, and he blazed the trail for his contemporaries and followers by the richness and variety of his [musical] inventions.

While the music to this song sounds more like a lullaby than a fight song, the meaning of the comic words were not lost on fifteenth-century listeners.

The Burgundian School

As one of the most celebrated musicians of his day, Dufay inspired his contemporaries, especially those in his home region of Burgundy. The Burgundian composers were noted for their sophisticated chansons, which were written for three-part harmony.

The Burgundian school of music developed in Dijon, France. The center of the Burgundian school was the court of Duke Philip the Good, and later that of his son Charles the Bold. Philip was a devoted patron of the musical arts and in 1506 employed as many as thirty-three court musicians—more than the powerful king of France. These players were singers,

Instruments of the Renaissance

In The Reformation, *Will Durant describes the musical instruments of the Renaissance Era:*

Although nearly all music in this age was vocal, the accompanying instruments were as diverse as in a modern orchestra. There were string instruments like psalteries, harps, dulcimers . . . lutes, and viols; wind instruments like flutes, oboes, bassoons, trumpets, trombones, cornets, and bagpipes; percussion instruments like drums, bells, clappers, cymbals, and castanets; keyboard instruments like organs, clavichords, harpsichords, spinets, virginals; there were many more. . . . Every educated home had one or more musical instruments, and some homes had special cabinets to hold them. Often they were works of art, fondly carved or fancifully formed, and they were handed down as treasures and memories from generation to generation. Some organs were as elaborately designed as Gothic cathedral fronts. . . . The organ was the chief but not the only instrument used in churches; flutes, pipes, drums, trombones, even kettledrums might add their incongruous summons to adoration.

The favorite accompaniment for the single voice was the lute. . . . Usually its body was made of wood and ivory, and shaped like a pear; its belly was pierced with holes in the pattern of a rose; it had six—sometimes twelve—pairs of strings, which were plucked by the fingers; its neck was divided by frets of brass into a measured scale, and its pegbox was turned back from the neck. When a pretty girl held a lute in her lap, strummed its strings, and added her voice to its tones, Cupid could save an arrow. . . .

The viol differed from the lute in having its strings stretched over a bridge and played by a bow, but the principle was the same—the vibration of taut struck strings over a box perforated to deepen sound. . . . During the sixteenth century the viola da braccio evolved into the violin, and in the eighteenth the viol passed out of use.

virtuoso instrumentalists, and composers. Philip the Good was devoted to secular music, and the musicians often played loud instruments made for the outdoors such as bagpipes, trumpets, tambourines, primitive oboes, lutes, flutes, harps, and an early incarnation of the viol, known as the *veille*.

Like most other rulers of the day, the duke was politically ruthless but, unlike many noblemen, a playful man in his own court. This was seen in 1454 at the Feast of the Pheasant when Philip had his court musicians play while seated in a huge pie dish. Mann speculates, "this event [might] have been the inspiration for the English nursery rhyme *Sing a song of sixpence* with its "four and twenty blackbirds/baked in a pie./When the pie was opened/the birds began to sing."[23]

Gilles Binchois

Although he never played in a pie dish, one of the foremost composers of the Burgundian School was Gilles Binchois, a contemporary of Dufay. A singer and composer from Mons, Belgium, Binchois wrote more than fifty chansons for solo voice and two instruments. Many of these are quite advanced for their time, with the voice singing the melody line, the lowest instrument playing a droning sort of note, and the middle instrument completing the three-part harmonic chord.

Like Dufay, Binchois was one of the most influential composers of the era, and his music was reproduced and played across Europe while other writers drew upon his works for inspiration. As Mann writes, "Binchois was particularly loved as a person . . . his joyous personality is mentioned more than once, and when he died he was commemorated in musical laments . . . by Dufay and the greatest composer of the next generation, Jean Ockeghem."[24]

The Netherlands School

Jean Ockeghem was from a new generation of composers who wrote between 1450 and 1550 during the era of flowering creativity referred to as the High Renaissance. These men were from the area in present-day Netherlands, Belgium, and northeastern France, hence this period is known as the "Netherlands School," or "the age of the Netherlanders."

Guillaume Dufay (left), a great master of the Burgundian school, is pictured with his contemporary Gilles Binchois, another gifted composer of the era.

The music of the Netherlands School was inspired by the works of Dufay and Binchois. It was expanded upon by Ockeghem, who was known as the Prince of Music for his technical mastery of musical forms such as motet, religious masses, and secular chansons. He utilized intricate four-part harmony, dramatic vocal bass parts, and complex counterpoint to write puzzle-like compositions that could only be played by the most skilled musicians. Such pieces inspired later Renaissance composers to use Ockeghem's innovative masterpieces as a foundation for their own musical explorations. When Ockeghem died, his life was celebrated in a musical lament written by one of his students, Josquin des Prez, another revered composer of the Netherlands School.

Josquin des Prez was French, but he worked for some of Italy's most powerful men in Milan, Rome, and elsewhere. The time spent in Italy colored his technically proficient Netherlands School music, giving it a more lighthearted sound that later came to be associated with all Renaissance music. As Alec Harmon writes in *Man and His Music Part 1: Mediaeval and Early Renaissance Music*:

> The impact of Italian culture . . . and the taste of [Josquin's] noble patrons . . . had a profound effect on the composer. It was as if the southern sun had warmed and stirred the closed bud of his genius, causing it to unfurl until the full flower was revealed. From now on, not only did he excel in all branches of vocal composition, but surpassed all other composers [of the Netherlands School] before the late sixteenth century in the range and quality of his feeling and imagination. . . . This emotional [music], expressed through sensuous harmony and melodic lines . . . of great beauty . . . together with a profound technical skill . . . make him . . . one of the greatest composers of all time.[25]

Josquin was among many composers who were renowned for their work in the sixteenth century, including Heinrich Isaac, Clément Janequin, and Orlande de Lassus. In Italy, Giovanni de Palestrina

The poems of Petrarch were set to music in sixteenth-century madrigals.

wrote such exquisite masses for unaccompanied voices that, like Ockeghem, he was known as the "Prince of Music."

Madrigals

Celebrated composers, such as Josquin, wrote complex music for kings, queens, and popes. But madrigals—songs written for three or more voices to sing in harmony without musical accompaniment—were extremely popular among average citizens in England, Italy, Spain, and elsewhere.

Like other "new" fashions of the Renaissance, madrigals are actually taken from an old style. In this case, they are based on poems written by fourteenth-century Italian poet Petrarch that were meant to be sung to music. These songs, originally called *frottole*, are stilted and repetitious, however. Many northern composers felt that the *frottole* did not do musical justice to Petrarch's sonnets and so revived the madrigal, which according to Mann is "a more flexible, expressive and emotional sort of music,"[26] therefore more fitting for Petrarch's verse.

The new madrigals, now with new verses, lacking refrains and other defining characteristics, little resemble their fourteenth-century namesakes. The term is used nonetheless for sixteenth-century songs sung by three to seven unaccompanied voices. Moving beyond the words of Petrarch, the subject matter of the madrigals is often an emotional mix of love, sex, and death. The rhythms of the music strongly emphasize words such as "anger" and "die" in what is known as "word painting."

The compositions of prominent English madrigalist William Byrd have survived for centuries.

In 1542 a book of five-voice madrigals written by Cipriano de Rore was published in Italy. As Grout writes, "Rore's preference for serious poetry of high literary quality set a standard for all subsequent madrigal composers."[27] After that time composers, imitating Rore, began to set the classic words of Virgil and Dante to music while adding emotion. They did this by pumping up robust harmonies with dissonant chords, that is, moody sounding notes that do not fit within the song's key.

Soon the madrigal appeared in England where it was tremendously well received. A lighter, less sophisticated version of the madrigal, known as the ballett, was also popular. It has repetitive verses and a sung "fa-la-la" refrain. For example, the leading English madrigalist William Byrd's "May" reads, "Now is the month of may-ing / When merry lads are play-ing / fa-la la la la la la la, fa-la la la la la la."[28]

Byrd's madrigals, along with so many others, are part of the Renaissance tradition that has survived throughout the centuries. While sounding quaint to modern ears, the music, like the era in which it was played, was revolutionary. On a cultural and social level the music grew and changed with the times, from serious liturgical masses to rollicking bawdy chansons and madrigals. As Durant concludes in *The Renaissance:*

> The great musical feature of the Renaissance was not theory, nor even technical advances; it was the increasing secularization of music. In the sixteenth century it was no longer religious music that made the advances and experiments; it was the music of the madrigal and the courts. Side by side with philosophy and literature, and reflecting the [ancient Greek] aspect of Renaissance art and the relaxation of morals, the music of sixteenth-century Italy escaped from [religious] control, and sought inspiration in the poetry of love.[29]

Chapter Three

The Baroque Era

B y the time the Renaissance era ended in 1600, music was an everyday part of life for Europeans from Italy in the south to England in the north. Classical music styles, however, were dominated by the intricate polyphonic music written by composers of the Netherlands School.

In Italy musicians had an increasing desire to move beyond the cold technical composition style of the Netherlanders. In an effort to inject emotional feelings such as joy, sadness, and anger into music, they experimented with different ways to achieve these effects.

By writing songs that suddenly changed speed, composers found that they were able to convey emotions through music. This effect was heightened by using a wider variety of instruments for tone color. For the first time, large orchestras were assembled so that the music could convey a broad range of feelings. In addition, simple song words were added so that audiences could easily understand emotional dramas expressed in song. These elements blended together in a style known as baroque, and were also prominent in opera, a new musical form that began to develop at the end of the 1500s.

Critical Words

The baroque era lasted from approximately 1600 to 1750, but the term itself is an odd choice for the musical flowering that took place during that time. In English, the word "baroque" is derived from the Italian *barocco,* meaning "bizarre." This may be traced back to the Portuguese term *barroco,* a word used for an irregularly shaped or misshapen pearl.

The word was originally applied to music in the 1730s by French poet Jean Baptiste Rousseau who scornfully mocked one composer as having written a piece that used "baroque chords of which so many idiots are enamoured." [30] Again, in the 1750s, Rousseau criticized Italian composers, saying that they wrote music that was "bizarre and

French poet Jean Baptiste Rousseau was the first to use the term "baroque" to describe the music of the early 1700s.

baroque." [31] The term was finally immortalized in the 1760s when Rousseau wrote a widely read dictionary of music in which he defined "baroque" as music "in which harmony is confused, charged with modulations and dissonances, in which the melody is harsh and little natural, intonation difficult and the movement constrained." [32] Critics of baroque music such as Rousseau believed it was overdone, clumsy, and strange.

Despite this dubious beginning, by the nineteenth century the original meaning of the term had been forgotten,

and baroque came to mean the elaborate and highly decorative art, architecture, and music from the period that followed the Renaissance and lasted until Johann Sebastian Bach died in 1750.

Expressing Emotion

The early baroque period was influenced by Italian concepts of emotional expression. Music was now altered in an attempt to express the dramatic themes of love, grief, anger, and sorrow. As Sadie and Latham write, "serenity and perfection of form [of the previous Renaissance era were] overtaken by the urgency of the expression of feeling." [33]

To express drama, baroque era composers wrote music that highlighted different feelings. For example, a loud fast passage might excite the audience and convey the emotions of joy, enthusiasm, or anger, depending on the piece. This section might end suddenly only to be followed by a quiet slow movement that leaves listeners sitting on the edges of their seats straining to hear the music. Here feelings of grief, peace, or suspense might well up among the audience. To heighten the emotional content or bring other feelings to the fore, movements might also alternate between loud and soft. For example trumpets might play brash melody notes while soft soothing oboes followed a bass line.

In a more complex display of contrast, one section of the orchestra, such as the woodwinds, might play a slow somber movement while another section, such as the strings, would play a rapid cascade of notes at the same time. This could express a feeling of manic behavior, or an eerie frightening sound.

At this time, music with such obvious contrasting elements was known as concerto. (Later, concerto was taken to mean a virtuoso musician playing a contrasting solo over the rest of the orchestra.) Taken to its extreme, the expression of contrasting musical emotions is known as monody, described by George J. Buelow in *The Late Baroque Era:*

> The new type of solo song, monody, became the particular love of performers and audiences, and monodies were written by the hundreds in the early decades of the [seventeenth] century. . . . Many monody texts were love-poems in which the . . . expectation and disappointment of the lover . . . were the [excuse] for . . . emotional . . . singing.[34]

Opera—a Fable in Music

The development of monody led a group of men to lay the groundwork for modern opera in Florence, Italy. In the late sixteenth century, about a dozen poets, writers, musicians, and composers, known as *camerata,* or "men who meet in a chamber," gathered at the palace of a local count with the goal of reviving ancient Greek drama in which tragedies were acted out in song and dance from the stage. David Ewen describes the work of the *camerata:*

The members of the *camerata . . .* felt strongly that if sixteenth-century Florentine poets were to write plays in the true spirit of Greek dramas, the texts must be supplied with music. This addition posed [a large] problem. After all, the prevailing music style of the time was still polyphony, and polyphony was . . . [not effective in] presenting [an understandable song]. You cannot have several people sing at the same time throughout a work and have the audience comprehend the words.

Actors perform in an ancient Greek drama. Opera began as a means of reviving Greek tragedies using song and dance.

And so, the *camerata* devised a new music style of one solo voice singing in a form of exaggerated speech. . . . Thus the *camerata* invented the monophonic, or monodic, style, which involved one voice reciting or declaiming in almost a speaking style. This singing-speaking style, called *stile rappresentativo* [theater style], was probably close to what we hear in opera today as recitative. . . . [A] simple instrumental accompaniment was used as a background for recitatives. By [1602] the style officially came to be known as "the new music" (*le nuove musiche*), a term . . . used as the title of a series of madrigals . . . [that] was devised to permit the performer "to speak through music."[35]

Working with the idea of speaking through music, composer Jacopo Peri created the first opera in 1597 from a story called *Dafne* which was based on ancient Greek mythology. The score is in the monodic style, and, as the term "opera" had not yet come into use, *Dafne* was referred to as a "fable in music," or "drama through music."[36] (The term opera came into common use in the early 1600s. It is taken from the Latin word for "work" as in "work of art.")

The new combination of drama and music was an instant success, and within a few years Peri was hired by King Henry IV of France to write another opera, this one for the royal wedding. This production, called *Euridice,* also is based on Greek mythology and features the character Orpheus.

While Peri is credited with writing the first musical dramas, his work has little resemblance to operas of later years. As Ewen says, Peri's work "is primitive by any standards. The text is naïvely conceived. . . . Most of the singing is . . . little more than stylized speech."[37]

The Triumph of Monteverdi

Within a few years the nobility grew tired of the slow wooden droning of Peri's work, and opera might have died a short time after its birth were it not for the genius of Claudio Monteverdi, born in 1567 in Cremona, Italy. Monteverdi was a virtuoso violin player and wrote his first madrigals when only seventeen. By the time he was in his early twenties, he was playing viol and violin in the palace orchestra of the Duke of Mantua.

Working with the court poet in Mantua, Monteverdi's first opera, *La Favola d'Orfeo (The Fable of Orpheus),* premiered in February 1607. Ewen praises the opera: "It was a triumph. The audience could not fail to be stirred by the drama, made so compelling through Monteverdi's music. . . . Through great tonal leaps in the vocal line (sometimes to express grief, sometimes excitement), Monteverdi intensifies the emotions."[38]

In addition to the unique vocal arrangements, Monteverdi's musical score calls for a wide variety of instru-

Attending the First Opera

In Opera, *David Ewen describes the scene in Florence at the end of the sixteenth century at the premier of* Dafne, *the first opera ever produced.*

That performance took place during the carnival of 1597. The auditorium was a brilliantly lit salon in [composer] Jacopo Corsi's palace. The splendor of this setting was hardly more awesome than the social position of the audience, all of whom were of the nobility, come by invitation. Backstage, the composer was putting on his costume, for in his opera he was assuming the role of Apollo.

The curtains parted. An old Greek legend, its theme the last word in ingenuousness, came to life. Dafne (or Daphne) is pursued by the god Apollo. To protect Dafne, her mother transforms the girl into a laurel tree, which then becomes sacred to Apollo. That's the whole story.

Surely the production would have been unremarkable, but for one important fact. The three characters—Dafne, Apollo, and Dafne's mother—*sang* rather than spoke their lines. The monotony of continuous recitatives was occasionally relieved by a dance or a brief choral number, the latter also in a monodic style. Further interest was contributed by the fact that the voices and the dances were accompanied by instruments: a harpsichord (the precursor of the piano) or organ, lutes, old-time flutes, and a bass viol (forerunner of the cello).

This new art form for the stage made a profound impression on its first audience. During the next two years *Dafne* was performed at the annual carnivals. Each time it was received with the greatest enthusiasm.

ments, unheard of at the time. In fact, *Orfeo* has been called the first use of a modern-type orchestra. At the beginning of the score, Monteverdi listed the instruments he required for the opera, according to Sadie and Latham: "Two harpsichords, two small wooden organs and a reed organ, a harp, two large lutes, three bass viols, ten violins and two small violins, two instruments like small double basses, four each of trumpets and trombones, two cornetts and two recorders."[39]

In the years after the debut of *Orfeo* Monteverdi became one of the most respected composers of the day.

Professional musicians throughout Italy learned to perform his works. As a result, opera became more accessible to average citizens, and dozens of public theaters were built for the first time. For example, there were no opera houses in Venice in 1630 but by 1637 there were a dozen. This, in turn, influenced baroque music across Europe as composers in Germany, England, and France began to write Italian-style operas to please the nobles who employed them, as Buelow explains:

> During the first three quarters of the [seventeenth] century, Venetian opera became the catalyst for the development of Baroque musical styles. . . . [By] the end of the century [opera] had become the most important and popular type of musical entertainment in the German courts, in the city of Hamburg, at the court of [French king] Louis XIV and, in the early eighteenth century, in London. Viewed from one perspective the history of the late Baroque [music] unfolds through the impact of operatic styles and forms on all music, sacred and secular.[40]

Baroque and Keyboard Music

While the popularity of secular opera was widespread, a school of mostly religious baroque music—based on the organ keyboard—flourished simultaneously in present-day Germany and other northern European locales. Pipe organs

In the mid-1500s, Claudio Monteverdi's compositions enriched opera as an art form, allowing it to flourish.

are large, expensive, and complicated instruments. Nevertheless, almost every middle-sized or large church owned an organ by the late 1600s. These churches employed organists who were expected to write compositions for services.

One of the most versatile organists of the baroque era was Dietrich Buxtehude, born in Denmark in 1637. Buxtehude spent most of his life in Lübeck in Northern Germany where he gave public concerts at Saint Mary's Church. These recitals attracted musicians from towns and villages throughout Germany. In fact, the renowned composer Johann Sebastian Bach, who was employed as a church organist, attended one of Buxtehude's concerts in 1705 and studied with him for four months.

Buxtehude was famous for his oratorios, long works for voice, chorus, and orchestra, often based on Biblical texts. Other compositions include choral works based on traditional Lutheran hymns. Perhaps the works that most impressed Bach were Buxtehude's toccatas—brilliant pieces of rapid music designed to let the organist show off his technique and touch on the keyboard.

The Musical Bachs

Buxtehude had a profound influence on Johann Sebastian Bach who, himself, is revered as the master of baroque music. Ironically, throughout his lifetime, Bach remained a regional composer and was little known outside of Germany. Even there he was mainly recognized not as a composer but as an organ virtuoso— and an organ designer and repairman.

When Johann Sebastian was born in the central German state of Thuringia on March 21, 1685, the Bach family already had produced several generations of well-known skilled musicians. In fact, because there were at one point thirty Bachs working as organists in Germany, the name Bach came to be used interchangeably with the word "musician" in the region.

Coming from such a large musical family, Johann Sebastian learned to play violin as soon as he could hold the instrument, and by the time he was a

Johann Sebastian Bach (at harpsichord) and his large family gather for morning prayers. Bach, a composer and musician of astonishing ability, came from a family of well-known musicians.

teenager he could sing and play organ, harpsichord, and other keyboard instruments. (The piano was not invented until around 1710, and such an instrument probably did not reach Germany until Bach was around twenty-five years old.)

Despite his talents, Bach, like many other gifted musicians, did not have an easy time of it. As Sherman and Seldon write, "He had to kiss up to his bosses to hold a job, he got in constant trouble with the authorities [for his musical experimentation], and when he wasn't turning out cantatas (more than 400 of them), he was producing children—at least 20 of them (although 13 of them died in infancy)."[41]

Bach's first brush with authorities critical of his music came after he had spent four months studying with Buxtehude. Bach's experience had given him exciting new melodic ideas that he played for the surprised and bewildered congregation upon returning to work as the church organist in Arnstadt. The composer was called before the church council and reprimanded, first for his four-month absence, and also for his new style of playing which went against the strict traditional styles practiced in church. The words of the council were recorded in Charles Sanford Terry's *Johann Sebastian Bach:*

Complaints have been made . . . that you now accompany the hymns with surprising variations and irrelevant ornaments, which obliterate the melody and confuse the congregation. If you desire to introduce a theme against the melody, you must go on with it and not immediately fly off to another. And under no circumstances must you introduce a *tonus contrarius* [tone conflicting with the melody].[42]

Bach was unhappy at Arnstadt and soon took another job as a church organist, this time in Mühlhausen where he began training the choir and a newly created orchestra to play his music. Bach was also assigned the task of restoring the organ he was assigned to play, for by this time he was also an expert on the mechanical workings of the complicated instrument.

Meanwhile, in 1708 Bach wrote a cantata (a vocal and instrumental piece composed of choruses and solos) called *Gott ist mein König (God Is My King)* to celebrate the inauguration of the town council. Sadly, *God is My King* is the only one of Bach's four hundred cantatas that was ever published in his lifetime.

Before long a religious controversy arose in Mühlhausen between the orthodox Lutherans, who were lovers of music, and the Pietists, who were very conservative and did not believe dramatic music should be played in church. Not wishing to be involved in this controversy, Bach resigned from his post on June 25, 1708.

"The Audacity of Genius"

The composer soon moved on to the small town of Weimar where the duke

In spite of Bach's great musical gifts, his duties as a court musician in Weimar also required him to wear a servant's uniform.

of Sachsen-Weimar offered him a position among his court chamber musicians. Following the trend of the baroque era, the court orchestra was large for its time, consisting of twenty-two musicians: a compact string ensemble, a bassoon player, six trumpeters, and a timpani player. Bach mainly played violin but he also filled in on harpsichord and wrote and arranged music. As was the custom in courts at that time, the musicians also spent time doing various household duties, and Bach, like the other musicians, was given a servant's uniform to wear.

At Weimar Bach was free to compose, and during this time he wrote many of his great organ works. When these pieces were published, Bach gained a well-deserved reputation throughout Germany as students flocked to his home to take lessons from the master.

Bach remained in the court orchestra for almost nine years. In 1717, however, when the duke's orchestra master, or Kapellmeister, died, Bach was passed over for the job, so instead spent the next five years as Kapellmeister for the young music-loving Prince Leopold at the small court of Cöthen.

In this idyllic atmosphere, Bach was completely devoted to music. He spent his days writing chamber music, violin concertos, sonatas, and keyboard music. He composed six concertos dedicated to Prince Christian Ludwig, margrave of Brandenburg. The *Brandenburg Concertos* are some of Bach's most famous compositions, and according to humanitarian and musicologist Albert Schweitzer in *J.S. Bach,*

In [the *Brandenburg Concertos*] we . . . have not one but several groups of solo instruments, that are played off against each other in the development of the movement. The wind instruments are used with the audacity of genius. In the first concerto Bach employs, besides the strings, a wind-*ensemble* consisting of two horns, three oboes and bassoon; in the second, flute, oboe, trumpet and violin are used as a

The Music of Bach

In The Complete Idiot's Guide to Classical Music *Robert Sherman and Philip Seldon list some of the greatest works of J.S. Bach.*

Almost everything Bach wrote is worthy of high attention, so where do we begin? Perhaps with the *Brandenburg Concertos,* those six magical works that were never performed during Bach's lifetime, but which are now an indelible part of 20th century concert life. Each one has its own special instrumental timbre: no. 2, for instance, has solo parts for flute, violin, oboe, and high trumpets; no. 3 is for strings alone; no. 5 features the harpsichord, and so forth.

Then try the two Violin Concertos and the Concerto for Two Violins; take an international sampling of keyboard pieces with the *French and English Suites* and the *Italian Concerto.* Listen to the six great sonatas and partitas for violin alone (the D Minor Partita contains the famous "Chaconne," one of the supreme achievements of the string repertoire).

On the vocal scene, take a few hours off and be inspired by the B Minor Mass; or for lighter listening, sip a bit of the *Coffee Cantata.* Bach was justly renowned for his mastery of counterpoint, but if you seek gorgeous melody, pure and simple, try "Sheep May Safely Graze" or "Jesu, Joy of Man's Desiring," the latter providing a spiritual uplift into the bargain.

kind of solo quartet against the body of the strings; in the third he aims at no contrast of *timbres,* but employs three string trios, all constituted in the same way; in the fourth concerto the concertino consists of one violin and two flutes; in the fifth it consists of clavier, flute and violin; in the sixth, Bach employs only the *timbre* effects to be had from the strings,—two violas, two gambas, and cello. [43]

While Bach may have had the "audacity of genius," in an ironic twist of fate, the margrave did not have the resources to hire an orchestra to play the *Brandenburg Concertos.* Bach was never able to hear the works performed during his lifetime.

Even after composing the concertos that would become one of the most beloved works of the nineteenth and twentieth centuries, Bach could not gain respect from church elders. When he applied for a job as music director at St. Thomas Church in Leipzig, he was passed over for another baroque composer, Georg Philipp Telemann. It was only after Telemann turned down the job that Bach was hired.

In Leipzig Bach was forced to take on a busy work schedule teaching singing classes, attending cantata rehearsals, overseeing Sunday and week-day services in the churches, and providing choirs for services in a local hospital and a prison. In spite of his workload, Bach provided a complete set of cantatas for every Sunday service for more than five years.

In 1727 Bach wrote *St. Matthew's Passion,* based on the Bible, in which characters such as Jesus, Peter, Pilate, and Judas all sing solos. A narrator tells the story and traditional hymns are mixed in between arias (solo vocal pieces). Although the works were relatively well received, Bach brought controversy upon himself in some quarters for making church music sound too much like opera. It was not until the nineteenth century that the genius of these pieces was recognized.

Today Bach is considered so important that musical historians have chosen the date of his death at the age of sixty-six, July 28, 1750, to mark the end of the entire musical era known as Baroque. But the greatness of his work was not fully realized until the beginning of the nineteenth century when composer Felix Mendelssohn revived *St. Matthew's Passion.* After that, Bach's surviving works were published and have been widely performed across the globe to this day.

Handel and Vivaldi

While Bach stands as the giant of baroque composers, he certainly was not the only genius of his time. George Frederic Handel, born in Saxony in 1685, received more recognition for his organ pieces—and far more money—than Bach. In fact, Handel was the personal composer to King George I of England and wrote his famous *Water Music Suite* so that the king would have something to listen to as he sailed up the Thames River. But, as Sherman and Seldon write, "Perhaps the crowning achievement of Handel's

Young George Frederic Handel is discovered in his family's attic late at night, exploring his musical talent.

life—certainly the work by which he is most often represented today—is *Messiah,* an oratorio he wrote in the incredibly short span of 24 days. We've all heard the great 'Hallelujah Chorus'; Handel said that when he wrote it, 'I saw all heaven before me, and the great God himself.'"[44]

Handel also was renowned for writing four operas including *Rinaldo* in 1711, *Julius Caesar* in 1724, *Partenope* in 1730, and *Serse* in 1738. While the composer's operatic work was respected, his output was small when compared to Antonio Vivaldi, born in Venice in 1648.

Although Vivaldi taught music in an all-girls orphanage his entire career, he found the time to compose forty operas as well as almost forty concertos for the bassoon alone. Drawing on the influence of Renaissance folk music, Vivaldi also

The Sonata

The sonata's musical form became popular during the baroque era. William Mann explains sonatas in James Galway's Music in Time.

A sonata is essentially music "sounded"—[that is] played, rather than sung (cantata). How long does a sonata last? Domenico Scarlatti's hundreds of harpsichord sonatas are in one short movement lasting about three minutes, generally written in contrasted pairs. Beethoven's *Hammerklavier* sonata for piano lasts over half an hour, some modern examples even longer. In Italy the sonata settled, during the seventeenth century, into a free-formed piece of several contrasted sections, usually for violin, or two violins, and continuo [a keyboard accompaniment]. A distinc-

tion was at first made between the *sonata da chiesa* (for performance in church) and the *sonata da camera* (to be played at court, perhaps in a cultured home): the former had four standard sections, slow-quick-slow-quick, the latter might include dance sections, as in a suite. By the early 1700s the distinction began to fade and the domestic sonata had acquired the same characteristics as the church variety.

It was [composer Arcangelo] Corelli . . . working in Rome, who, from 1681 standardized the number and length of the movements, which he kept separate. The keyboard solo sonata originated in Germany . . . as an instrumental work in several movements. The sonata travelled from Italy into Germany and other European countries.

wrote energetic and rhythmic concertos for mandolin, lute, and even guitar, as well as the more common flute, oboe, and violin.

Vivaldi's most famous work is *Four Seasons,* four concertos that musically illustrate the seasons. The work is expressive and playful, as Sherman and Seldon write: "Listen carefully . . . and you'll find a marvelous example of descriptive music, with clever images of twittering birds, burbling brooks, snoozing shepherds, chattering teeth, horses at the hunt, and pelting hailstorms."[45]

By the end of the baroque era composers such as Vivaldi, Handel, and Bach had transformed music from pieces written for small vocal and instrumental ensembles to orchestral and choral pieces that were grandiose, dramatic, and ornate. At the same time opera spread sophisticated music among all classes of people. From the simple monody of the post-Renaissance period to the glorious power of Handel's *Messiah,* baroque era composers left an indelible impression upon the history of music.

Chapter Four

The Classical Period

The classical era, between 1750 and 1820, was defined by the great composers who were famous during that period, and the names Mozart and Beethoven stand above all others in the pantheon of Western music. Other composers, however, such as Franz Joseph Haydn and Franz Peter Schubert also contributed mightily to the classical era.

While historians divide musical eras into neat categories, the music itself followed no such tidy timeline. Musicians of the classical era were influenced by those of the baroque era. For example, the music of Bach had a profound influence on those who followed, according to Sherman and Seldon:

Beethoven played several pieces from Bach's *Well-Tempered Clavier;* Chopin knew all forty-eight preludes and fugues by heart. Mozart made string transcriptions of Bach pieces and wrote to his father that he had finally found music with something to teach him. Perhaps [composer Hector] Berlioz summed it up best when he wrote to a friend that "Bach is Bach, just as God is God."[46]

While classical musicians were influenced by the past, they were also looking forward to a brighter future. The eighteenth century was an era of philosophical advances known as the Enlightenment. The philosophers of the Enlightenment were deeply influenced by scientific theories and strongly rejected the unbending religious dogma of the Church. They believed in human reason as opposed to religious miracles. They supported self-expression, free from censorship by church or state, while opposing religious intolerance and the repression of the people by the totalitarian kings and princes who ruled Europe. The philosophers of the Enlightenment dreamt of a society where truth would triumph over ignorance, reason over superstition, and where liberty and freedom would topple oppressive despotism.

The philosophies of the Enlightenment naturally affected artists, the arts, and their influence on the popular culture. The influence of the Enlightenment on classical music may be seen as a notable decline of religious compositions accompanied by a sharp rise in secular music written specifically for middle-class audiences rather than the nobility. This trend was promoted by philosophers who believed that art and music should be for everybody, not just a chosen few. Overall, this influenced classical composers to write music that was logical, intelligent, balanced, and embraced reason. Sadie and Latham explain how this affected opera:

[We] find, in the early eighteenth century, forms of opera arising that were given not only in foreign languages and private theaters but in native languages and in public. In France, the genre known as "opéra comique", in which songs were interspersed with spoken dialogue in simple stories about common folk, got decisively under way. . . . In England, while Italian opera entertained the London aristocratic audiences, a middle-class public enjoyed . . . lightweight operas with spoken dialogue, composed in a simple and tuneful style; these were performed not just in London but all over the country. In Germany, English operas of

this kind, translated and given in Berlin and Hamburg around the middle of the century, provoked the development of the native German form, the *Singspiel.* And in Italy, new forms of comic opera appeared . . . appealing with their popular subject-matter and their catchy melodies to a public that found the behavior of the classical and mythological figures of serious opera incomprehensible and their music boring. [47]

Wolfgang Amadeus Mozart (pictured) is one of the giants of Western classical music.

Simple, Elegant Music

While professionally composed music became more available to the general public, advances in music publishing and instrument manufacture allowed a growing class of amateur musicians to improve their skills. Serious composers found that if they could write music that was elegant and interesting—yet simple enough for amateurs to play—they could earn respectable incomes publishing their work in lesson books. Meanwhile songbooks from favorite operas were very popular among people who wanted to sing songs at home that they had enjoyed in the theater. By using these books, refined young women were expected to learn to play the piano or harpsichord while young men picked up the violin, oboe, or flute. Professional musicians augmented their incomes by giving lessons in peoples' homes.

This shift in music from the complex and mysterious to the simple and elegant was advanced by the form known as *style galant,* or galant [gallant] defined by Sadie and Latham:

"[*Style galant*] meant a flowing melodic [song], free of the complexities of counterpoint. . . . A galant melody . . . would normally be lightly accompanied . . . [by an] instrument (like the harpsichord) with a . . . slow-moving bass line that did nothing to draw attention away from the melody. The ideal medium for galant melody was the singing voice, in a cantata or an operatic song (preferably on an amorous text). . . . Another popular medium was

During the classical period, refined young women were expected to learn to play the piano or harpsichord.

the flute . . . which was specially esteemed for its capacity for elegant and tender shading.[48]

The Symphony Orchestra

To play *style galant,* orchestras composed of keyboards, woodwind, brass, string, and (occasionally) percussion sections were formed. Called symphony orchestras, these new configurations were one of the defining aspects of the classical era, and they played a new musical form called the symphony. *Style galant* could also be performed by another new orchestral configuration, the string quartet, composed of two violins, a cello, and a viola—a stringed instrument tuned an octave above the cello.

The word "symphony" comes from Greek and means "sounding together." Although most modern symphonies have four movements, the first symphony-like pieces are made up of just three songs, or movements, of various lengths. These symphonies are standardized into two styles: The three movements of symphonies written in the French style feature tempos played slow-quick-slow; Italian style is played quick-slow-quick. Most early symphonic composers, however, did not have organized orchestras to play their music and simply assembled whatever musicians were available when it was time to give a performance. This gave the music an amateurish sound produced by musicians who had little practice playing together.

This problem was solved in the mid-eighteenth century, when the foundation of the modern professional symphony was laid by violinist Johann Stamitz in the southern German city of Mannheim. Stamitz was hired by the city's music-loving ruler Carl Theodor to act as concertmaster in the Mannheim court. Stamitz, from what is now the Czech Republic, composed as many as seventy symphonies despite the fact that he died at the age of forty. And the symphonies of Stamitz became in-stantly popular throughout Europe, attracting so many composers and musicians to the southern German town that a class of music known as the Mannheim School grew up around his talents. Sherman and Seldon describe the sounds of Stamitz:

> [The] orchestra pioneered gradations of sound that had been unknown before—swellings of volume (crescendo) and its opposite (diminuendo), a kind of drooping figure that became known as the "Mannheim Sigh" and a leaping group of notes nicknamed the "Mannheim Rocket."

> Local composers, members of the so-called Mannheim School, wrote pieces to take special advantage of these exciting orchestral possibilities, and by showing the world what creative imagination, effective leadership, and high performing discipline could accomplish, the Mannheimers gave the symphony orchestra a completely new significance in the musical world.[49]

Because they were supported by nobility with somewhat limited funds, the symphony orchestras of the Mannheim era were much smaller than modern configurations which may have well over one hundred musicians. For example, in the mid-1750s the Mannheim orchestra had only forty-five members, and even by the end of the eighteenth century respected orchestras in major

Concert Life

With the Enlightenment, music became more accessible to the average person, and the first public concerts were performed in Europe, The Cambridge Music Guide *describes this phenomenon.*

It was in the eighteenth century that concert life began as we know it. In earlier times instrumental music was chiefly intended for performance at court or for groups of gentleman amateurs to play in their homes. Now a new phenomenon arose. Groups of people, often of both amateurs and professionals, got together to give concerts for their own pleasure . . . and for the pleasure of others who came to hear them. In larger cities, where more professionals were to be found, orchestral concerts were regularly given. London and Paris led, and others were quick to follow. The concerts of court orchestras were often opened to a paying public. During the late eighteenth century in particular, concert life developed rapidly; traveling virtuosos went from city to city, organizing concerts in each, while local musicians of repute often gave annual "benefit concerts" (from which they retained the takings). The orchestra as an entity began to take firm shape. The concept of a public that came to concerts to listen was a novel one, demanding a novel approach to composition; it was more than ever necessary for a piece of music to have a logical and clearly perceptible shape, so that it would grasp and hold the listener's attention and interest. Composers rose to this challenge: above all, the three great men of the era, Haydn, Mozart, and Beethoven.

cities such as Venice rarely had more than thirty-five players.

Franz Joseph Haydn— "Father of the Symphony"

While Stamitz may have been the originator of the modern symphony orchestra, Franz Joseph Haydn's huge contribution to the musical style earned him the name "Father of the Symphony."[50] Born in 1732 to an impoverished family in a small town in eastern Austria, Haydn spent almost thirty years in the position of Kapellmeister at a provincial court outside of Vienna. While working for Prince Nicholas "the Magnificent" Esterhazy, who owned twenty-one castles, Haydn spent most of his life in the prince's sumptuous two-hundred-room palace in the remote countryside of Eisenstadt.

From 1761 to 1790—the height of the classical era—Haydn conducted the twenty-five-member royal orchestra and a dozen singers while composing operas, chamber music, ceremonial pieces, and other works for the prince. In addition to writing about one original composition per week, the Kapellmeister's job required him to coach the singers, fix broken instruments, and make sure the musicians, some of the finest in Europe, were properly groomed and arrived at work on time. Since the prince played the viola-like baryton, Haydn composed over two hundred pieces for that stringed instrument.

Although his workload kept him busy, Haydn considered himself lucky to be able to write music continually without interruptions or restrictions. As the composer told his biographer before his death,

> My Prince was content with all my works, I received approval, I could, as head of an orchestra, make experiments, observe what enhanced an effect, and what weakened it, thus improving, adding to, cutting away, and running risks. I was set apart from the world, there was nobody in my vicinity to confuse and annoy me in my course, and so I had to be original.[51]

Haydn's isolation at the secluded palace enhanced his creative work. And while employed by the prince, Haydn's music was heard by the most powerful heads of state in Europe and beyond. As his fame spread, by the 1770s publishers were clamoring to print Haydn's music, which sold at a rapid rate.

The composer was so prolific at this time that he wrote an astounding 106

Franz Joseph Haydn is remembered as the "Father of the Symphony."

symphonies, 68 string quartets, 60 piano sonatas, 25 operas, 4 oratorios, and countless songs, arias, cantatas, overtures, concertos, serenades, trios, and chamber works.

Haydn was said to have had a sense of humor, possibly because of the names he gave his symphonies. For example, no. 83 is nicknamed *The Hen* because the first movement features

Haydn's Courtly Life

When Franz Joseph Haydn was hired to work for a German prince, he was given a set of royal instructions he was expected to follow to the letter. According to László Somfai in The Classical Era *(edited by Neal Zaslaw), Haydn had to "settle the quarrels of his musicians . . . look after the instruments . . . rehearse the expensively trained female singers . . . and so on." The original contract states even more conditions.*

His Serene Princely Highness is graciously pleased to place confidence in him, that as may be expected from an honourable house officer in a princely court, he will be temperate, and will know that he must treat the musicians placed under him not overbearingly, but with mildness and leniency, modestly, quietly and honestly . . . and the said Joseph [Haydn] . . . shall follow the instructions which have been given to them, appearing neatly in white stockings, white linen, powdered, and either with pigtail or hair-bag, but otherwise of identical appearance. . . .

[Haydn] shall appear daily (whether here in Vienna or on the estates) in the *antichambre* before and after midday, and inquire whether a high princely [order] for a musical performance has been given. . . .

The said . . . *Capel-Meister* shall be under permanent obligation to compose such pieces of music as his Serene Princely Highness may command, and neither to communicate such new compositions to anyone, nor to allow them to be copied, but to retain them wholly for the exclusive use of his Highness; nor shall he compose for any other person without the knowledge and gracious permission [of his Highness]. . . .

The party of the second part [Haydn] agrees to perform any music of one kind or another in all the places, and all the times, to which and when H. Highness is pleased to command.

Haydn is pictured here conducting a string quartet. He composed sixty-eight pieces for string quartets in his lifetime.

oboes and violins making "clucking" sounds. Mann lists the titles for some other symphonies and how they earned their names:

> [The] *Surprise,* no. 94 (a loud chord to awake sleepy listeners), the *Miracle,* no. 96 (a glass chandelier fell and broke in the concert-room, but hurt nobody because the audience, carried away by the power of the music, had crowded to the edge of the . . . [stage]) . . . ; *La Passione,* no. 49, one of Haydn's minor-key, high-[spirited] dramatic

works, later called his *Sturm und Drang* ("Storm and Stress") period. The *Farewell* symphony, no. 45 in F sharp minor, was composed as a reminder to the Prince that his musicians were impatient to return home to Vienna: in the finale, the players stop playing one by one, snuff out the candles on their music-desks and leave the platform, until finally only two solo violins are left playing in the extravagant key of F sharp major. The Prince is reported to have understood the message.[52]

While under the prince's patronage, Haydn had little idea of how famous and respected he was throughout Europe. When the prince died in 1790, however, Haydn traveled to London where he was hired by promoter Johann Peter Salomon to write a dozen new symphonies and conduct concerts. In England, the composer quickly became an instant celebrity. His concerts were so enthusiastically received that cheering and applauding audiences encouraged him to repeat entire movements.

After returning to Vienna, Haydn grew tired of writing symphonies but continued to compose songs, oratorios, string quartets, and even the Austrian national anthem. In 1805 a London newspaper mistakenly printed Haydn's obituary and England went into a period of mourning. The composer was forced to state that he was still alive, humbly writing, "How can I die now? . . . I have only just begun to understand the wind instruments."[53] In 1809, however, the master did die.

Although Haydn spent most of his life in a prince's palace isolated from the rest of society, his contribution is legendary, as his biographer Ernst Ludwig wrote in 1790:

When we speak of Joseph Haydn, we think of one of our greatest men: great in small things and even greater in large; the pride of our age. Always rich and inexhaustible; forever new and surprising, forever noble and great, even when he seems to laugh. He gave to our instrumental music, and in particular to quartets and symphonies, a perfection that never before existed.[54]

Mozart the Child Prodigy

In 1761 when Haydn first went to work for Prince Nicholas, another Austrian musician—Wolfgang Amadeus Mozart—was only five years old. Despite his tender age, the little Mozart was a budding musician. In fact he would write his first composition, "Symphony no. 1," the following year at age six.

Like Johann Sebastian Bach, Mozart was born into a musical family. His father, Leopold, was a composer and violinist for the respected thirty-eight-piece court orchestra in Salzburg. Leopold was married to Anna Maria Mozart and the couple had seven children, only two of whom survived: the fourth child, a daughter named Maria Anna Walburga Ignatia, called Nannerl; and the seventh and last child, a boy born on January 27, 1756. Leopold believed that this child was a miracle because he was so small and weak it did not seem that he would survive. They called him Wolfgang. His second name was Theophilus, meaning "loved by God," but Wolfgang preferred to use Amadeus, the Latin translation of his middle name.

Wolfgang showed musical talent at an incredibly young age. By the time he was three years old he could plunk out tunes on the piano, and his ears were so sensitive that loud noises would make him physically ill. The boy also had perfect pitch—the ability to name a note simply by hearing it—and at the age of four he was telling court musicians that their violins were a quarter tone out of tune. By that time, according to Mozart's first biographer Friedrich Schlichtegroll, Mozart could learn a minuet in thirty minutes "and then play it perfectly, cleanly, and with the steadiest rhythm."[55]

By the time the child was six, Leopold recognized that his young genius might be able to support the family with his talents. Nannerl, too, was a musical child prodigy, and so Leopold and his two children began an extensive tour of the royal courts, musical academies, and public concerts of Europe playing for imperial ministers, archdukes, emperors, and queens. As word spread of the young man's talents the Mozarts were invited to play in England, France, Germany, and elsewhere. During his travels the young boy met many famous musicians of the day, heard all styles of music from the many regions of the continent, and remembered them for use in his later compositions.

To enhance his musical shows Wolfgang would perform tricks taught to him by his father, such as playing complicated music on first sight, giving demonstrations of his perfect pitch, and playing a clavier keyboard that was covered by a cloth so he could not see the keys.

When Mozart traveled to Italy at the age of fourteen he was inspired to write his first opera, *Mitridate ré di Ponto,* which was performed in Milan in December 1770. *Mitridate* was enthusiastically received, as Leopold wrote in a letter to his wife: "God be praised, the first performance of the Opera . . . took place on the 26th amid general applause. . . . Never in living memory was such curiosity over a first Opera to be seen in Milan as this time."[56]

By the age of six, Mozart was considered a musical child prodigy.

The young composer continued to tour Europe, and by the time he returned to Italy in 1773, Mozart had written four Masses, two long operas and one short operetta, twelve choral works, and at least thirty symphonies, each about ten minutes long. In *The Lives of the Great Composers* music critic Harold C. Schonberg describes the talents of Mozart:

> There was literally nothing in music he could not do better than anybody else. He could write down a complicated piece while thinking out another piece in his head; or he could think out a complete string quartet and then write out the individual parts before making the full score; or he could read perfectly at sight any music placed before him; or he could hear a long piece of music for the first time and immediately write it out, note for note.[57]

"The Most Natural Musician"

Although Mozart was an incredibly gifted composer and musician, by the time he reached his late teens he was no longer a child prodigy who could attract standing-room-only crowds to his concerts. Unable to find work elsewhere, Mozart took a job as Kapellmeister for the archbishop of Salzburg where he was paid barely enough to survive, all the while composing operas, symphonies, oratorios, quartets, concertos, sonatas, and other works.

While Mozart was writing pieces that remain popular today, he garnered little respect—or financial gain—from his employers—or even the general public. During his twenties, the composer augmented his income giving lessons and publishing sonatas. Despite a constant shortage of funds, a rocky marriage, and the death of his mother, Mozart continued to write joyous, enduring music. From his pen flowed the *Coronation Mass,* the beautiful E-flat Concerto for two pianos, and the equally marvelous *Sinfonia Concertante* for violin, viola, and orchestra. In addition he received a major commission for the opera *Idomeneo* about the king of ancient Crete who returns home to many problems after fighting the Trojan War.

Tired of working for unappreciative bosses Mozart finally struck out on his own, working as one of the world's first "freelance" musicians—a job few other less famous composers could manage. He performed often as a solo virtuoso pianist and had a number of rich patrons who enjoyed his musical talents.

In 1782 Mozart wrote another comic opera, *The Abduction from the Seraglio,* about a Spanish nobleman who rescues his lover from a Turkish harem. The characters were dressed in Turkish costumes, which was considered exotic and exciting at that time, and the opera was an extraordinary success.

Working with Italian poet and lyricist Lorenzo da Ponte, Mozart wrote three immortal operas between 1786

A modern production of Mozart's operatic fantasy The Magic Flute. *It was the last composition he wrote before his death in 1791.*

and 1790—*The Marriage of Figaro, Don Giovanni,* and *Così fan tutte.* The first two were immediate successes when they were performed in Prague, and Mozart achieved the greatest widespread public acclaim of his career.

In 1791, working with actor Emanuel Schikaneder, Mozart wrote yet another comic opera, *The Magic Flute,* a fairy tale about a prince who tries to rescue a maiden. The opera featured clever tunes, special musical effects, witches, monsters, and other entertainments that made it a stunning success over the course of one hundred performances.

Soon after writing *The Magic Flute,* Mozart became ill with exhaustion and fever. At one o'clock in the morning on December 5, 1791, Wolfgang Amadeus Mozart died at the age of thirty-six. Although the exact cause of death remains unknown, modern researchers suggest that the composer suffered from kidney failure.

In the years after his death the world became aware of Mozart's musical genius, realizing that the composer excelled in all forms of music including opera, symphony, concerto, chamber music, vocal, piano, and choral music. By the age of twenty he had played virtuoso violin, was the best living pianist and organist in Europe, and was the finest conductor of his time. In his short thirty-six years of life he wrote more than six hundred extraordinary pieces of music and gave the world a legacy of music that many believe is still unsurpassed to this day. By the nineteenth century it was apparent to many that Mozart is, in the words of Harold C. Schonberg, "the most perfect, best equipped, and most natural musician the world has ever known."[58]

Beethoven

Along with Mozart, Ludwig van Beethoven is one of the giants of the classical era. Because of the emotional, expressive, and moody characteristics of his music, however, some of Beethoven's later music resembles that of the romantic era. Since he was influenced by classical composers and his music inspired the Romantics, Beethoven is sometimes described by musical historians as a "giant straddling two styles."[59]

Born on December 17, 1770, in the city of Bonn, then a part of the Austrian empire, Beethoven was from a musical family. His grandfather, also named Ludwig, was the Kapellmeister employed by the elector of Cologne. His father, Johann, was an uncelebrated tenor singer also employed by the elector. Johann wanted to make his son into a child prodigy like Mozart. Unfortunately the senior Beethoven was a violent alcoholic who beat Ludwig when he made musical mistakes—even after forcing the child to practice for hours on end.

Although he never achieved the kind of childhood fame that Mozart had obtained, at the age of seventeen Ludwig journeyed to Vienna where he was lucky enough to take a few lessons from Mozart, who was a rising star at that time. After excitedly playing a piece for Mozart, the older composer told his friends about Beethoven, "Keep your eyes on him; some day he will give the world something to talk about."[60]

Beethoven also took lessons from Haydn and so was able to meet many Viennese aristocrats. The young man began to make a name for himself playing at fashionable private parties. Beethoven took to improvising—making up the music as he played it—which thrilled his wealthy patrons. In fits of musical passion, Beethoven would smash his hands down on the keyboard so hard he would break piano strings. In 1838 Ferdinand Ries, a friend of Beethoven's and his first biographer, wrote about the pianist's improvisational style: "All the artists I ever heard improvise did not come anywhere near the heights reached by Beethoven in his discipline. The wealth of ideas which poured forth, the moods to which he surrendered himself, the variety of interpretation, the complicated challenges which evolved or which he introduced were inexhaustible."[61]

Despite performing for formally dressed, upper-class audiences, Beethoven seldom took care of his appearance, and his hair was always wild and unruly. His moods changed constantly and his friends never knew when a chance remark might be taken the wrong way, sending the pianist into fits of rage. While Beethoven was difficult to get along with, the nobility flocked to hear his music, and the composer's future looked bright. Compositions flowed from him and he toured often, giving concerts in Prague, at the royal court of Prussia in Berlin, and in other important European cities.

Young Beethoven plays for Mozart (center) and others of Vienna's musical elite. Beethoven took lessons from Mozart while in Vienna.

Beethoven's Torment

When Beethoven was a child, his father often beat him around the ears, permanently damaging his hearing. By the time he was thirty, the great composer began to lose his ability to hear. Beethoven writes of his torment in a letter to his friend Franz Wegeler, quoted by Alexander Thayer in The Life of Ludwig van Beethoven, *vol. 1.*

[M]y] ears whistle and buzz continually day and night. I can say I am living a wretched life; for two years I have avoided almost all social gatherings because it is impossible for me to say to people: "I am deaf." If I belonged to any other profession it would be easier, but in my profession it is an awful state, the more since my enemies, who are not a few, what would they say? In order to give you an idea of this singular deafness of mine I must tell you that in the theatre I must get very close to the orchestra in order to understand the actor. If I am a little distant I do not hear the high tones of the instruments, singers, and if I be but a little farther away I do not hear at all. Frequently I can hear the tones in a low conversation, but not the words, and as soon as anybody shouts, it is intolerable. It seems that in conversation there are people who do not notice my condition at all, attributing it to my absent-mindedness. Heaven knows what will happen to me. . . . I have often cursed my existence . . . there will be moments in my life when I am the unhappiest of God's creatures.

By 1800 the composer was in his prime, writing the famous *Pathétique* sonata which was one of the first pieces written in the romantic style that would become the hallmark of the nineteenth century. In addition, Beethoven wrote five piano sonatas, three violin sonatas, two cello sonatas, the Trio in B-flat Major, six string quartets, a quintet, chamber music, and songs including the famous "Adelaide."

The year 1800 also was marked by the first performance of Beethoven's First Symphony. In 1801 Beethoven wrote the music for the ballet *The Creatures of Prometheus,* which was performed many times in Vienna. Among other works written that year were the famous pieces known as *The Funeral March* (Piano Sonata opus 26) and the *Moonlight Sonata* (Piano Sonata opus 27).

While creating enduring works of music, Beethoven began to lose his hearing when he was around thirty years old. Despite this handicap the composer carried on, writing symphonies in what has been called "the heroic style" for their timeless and dramatic quality. As Mann writes: "Beethoven wanted his audience to regard music not as the entertainment accepted by earlier audiences, but as some sort of sermon about the godlike nature of man."[62]

Beethoven's third through eighth symphonies are triumphant displays of the composer's genius written, ironically, when he was almost completely deaf. Sherman and Seldon describe Beethoven's work during this so-called Middle Period in the composer's life: "Beethoven embarked on a revolutionary path. From here on, he would experiment with new forms even as he was expanding the old ones, invent his own musical parameters, produce works on a vast and heroic scale, and

Beethoven began to go deaf at age thirty, a tragic circumstance for the composer.

ultimately shatter existing preconceptions about the expressive potential of music altogether."[63]

Although he spent most of the later years of his life in self-imposed isolation, Beethoven continued to write, often while laying his head on the piano, straining to feel the vibrations of the notes. When he finally died at the age of fifty-six, the composer's death was as dramatic as his music.

At 5:45 P.M. on March 26, 1827, a large clap of thunder rocked Vienna and a flash of lightning filled the room where Beethoven was lying sick and unconscious. A man named Anselm Hüttenbrenner, who was with the composer at that moment, wrote, "After this unexpected phenomenon of nature . . . Beethoven opened his eyes, lifted his right hand and looked up several seconds with his fist clenched and a very serious, threatening expression. . . . When he let the raised hand sink to the bed, his eyes closed half-way. . . . Not another breath, not another heartbeat more!"[64]

Several days later, his funeral procession through the streets of Vienna attracted twenty thousand people who came to say good-bye to the man who would someday be recognized as one of the greatest musical geniuses of the nineteenth century.

While the extraordinary symphonic gifts of Haydn, Mozart, and Beethoven dominated the classical era, they were joined by other men who also made lasting contributions. But it was the opening "Da-da-da-dummmm" chords of Beethoven's Fifth and the lilting melodies of Mozart's *Magic Flute* that continue to define the classical period nearly two centuries later.

Chapter Five

The Romantic Era

At the beginning of the nineteenth century, music was dominated by the three geniuses of the classical era—Haydn, Mozart, and Beethoven. Almost every other composer who hoped to earn a living writing music attempted to reproduce the symphonic styles pioneered by these towering giants. Not every composer, however, was content to imitate what some considered the dry formal styles of great masters. Inspired by earth-changing events such as the American and French Revolutions in the last quarter of the eighteenth century, a new generation of composers began to experiment with innovative musical ideas that were also considered revolutionary.

The new music was called romantic, a term also used to describe the literary style of the day. Romantic composers often used books, poems, or plays as inspiration for their music and even incorporated the written word into musical pieces. The leading author of the romantic movement was Johann Wolfgang Von Goethe, whose books stress human passions, imagination, and freedom. This was a departure from the classical style that embraced logic, intellect, reason, balance, and form. Several operas were based on the romantic works of Goethe such as *Faust,* that told of a man who sold his soul to the devil in trade for immortality and love from an unattainable woman.

The Romantics ignored the rigid musical rules of the classical era and composed pieces that were emotional, expressive, and moody. In opera the focus shifted to medieval tales of the supernatural complete with evil spirits, witches, and soul-snatching demons. In addition to old-fashioned morality tales, romantic music was inspired by real-world political events of the eighteenth century. After Napoleon took over France in 1790 he attempted to conquer all of Europe, and the Napoleonic Wars, which lasted until 1815, created misery across the continent. When the French

Emperor was defeated there was a rising tide of nationalism in European countries. People became very devoted, sometimes fanatically so, to the cultures and accomplishments of their homelands. This was reflected in the music of the romantic era, as Sherman and Seldon write:

> [There was a] turn toward works that evoked pride in the creator's homeland. Composers in the Romantic era took special note of traditions in their native countries, giving symphonic life to country folk tunes and rustic dance rhythms, painting tonal landscapes of rivers, mountains, and castles, bringing national poetry and other literary works to bear on their musical instincts. Thus we find classical pieces deriving from local legends . . . nature sketches . . . or historical personages.[65]

The Lied and the Tone Poem

The musical celebration of folktales, national pride, and natural wonders defines the romantic era. Inspired by literature and the visual arts, this was a

The passionate style of the author Goethe (pictured) led several romantic composers to adapt his works as operas.

Romantic Music

In Classical Music for Everybody *Dhun H. Sethna compares classical and romantic music styles.*

Classic and Romantic . . . [relate] to the two basic instincts of human nature: on the one hand, the need to control and moderate the emotions and, on the other, to express an . . . emotional longing for the forbidden, the unknown and the unattainable. [Where] the Classical aroused [feelings of rest] and serenity, the . . . Romantic suggested restlessness and disorder. Eternal longing, regret for the lost happiness of childhood, or . . . [discontent] gnawed at the soul and formed the ingredients of the Romantic spirit. . . . [Where] the Classical had found inspiration in the gods and heroes of ancient Greece, the Romantics discovered the Dark Ages . . . fairy tales and medieval sagas, folk dances and nationalism. Here were the great themes of the triumph of good over evil, of God and nature, of life and death and man's destiny, and of the struggle for freedom. In its music it found expression in the great heaven-storming climaxes, the violent contrasts between deafening loudness and a whispering softness, and in [touching] melodies. . . .

Here was a new spirit of individualism, a sense of uniqueness: If the Romantic was not any better than his fellow man, at least he considered himself different.

time of glorifying the fantastic, the bizarre, the beautiful, the emotional, and the creative. This allowed composers a new freedom to put aside the formal structures of the past and explore a unique approach to music. For example, composers might utilize dissonant chord progressions that did not fit with the rest of the piece, or rely on a long drawn-out solo by a distinctive-sounding instrument even if it interrupted the natural flow of the symphony.

Another hallmark of the romantic era involved the pairing of music and words. Goethe himself was a musician who created poetry that was specifically written to be set to music. Beethoven and others wrote compositions based on Goethe's words. These are called art songs or "lieder" (pronounced leeder) in German. Franz Schubert was the leader of the lied, writing an incredible 145 songs in the eighteenth year of his life. Before his untimely death at the age of thirty-one, Schubert wrote more than six hundred lieder, seventy of them based on the poems of Goethe. In *Music Through the Ages,* Marion Bauer and Ethel P. Peyser describe the lieder of Schubert:

> His piano accompaniments are unique in their collaboration with the voice. The simple, broken chords of "The Meadow Rose" convey the innocence and serenity of the poem. With a measure or two, we can "hear" the babbling brook in which the trout swim. And in the agitated . . . [notes], against which sounds a foreboding bass . . . the eerie atmosphere of Goethe's . . . [story] is firmly established.[66]

Schubert's moody lieder inspired some romantic composers to do away with the words altogether and attempt to tell stories with sounds alone. These are called "tone poems," or symphonic poems—orchestral works based on literature that tells an often complicated tale through music. These pieces might inspire listeners to imagine fields, forests, or other landscapes or else think of specific characters from a novel or poem. The most complex tone poems try to convert complete stories to musical sounds.

The Contradictions of Schumann

One of the most gifted creators of tone poems was Robert Schumann, born in Saxony in 1810. Schumann learned to play the piano as soon as he was tall enough to reach the keys while standing on a chair. By the age of eleven he was directing his school band. As he grew older Schumann fell in love with literature and wrote poems, stories, and even several novels, all of which remained unfinished.

After penning his first musical compositions in the early 1830s, Schumann became editor in chief of the magazine *New Journal of Music* in Leipzig, a position he held from 1835 to 1845. The journal was a leading proponent of the romantic school of music, and Schumann wrote satirical essays about a fictional group of musicians who, according to Bauer and Peyser, "were fighting against the musical Philistines [smug, ignorant people]. It was a struggle of a new order against the old; of the ultra-modern Romanticism against the decadent Classicism; of the youthful, subjective, and emotional against the artificial and [dull]."[67] In the pages of his magazine Schumann sang the praises of relatively unknown (at the time) romantic geniuses such as Frédéric Chopin, Johannes Brahms, Schubert, and others.

In addition to his magazine work Schumann published dozens of piano compositions. These song cycles such as "Viennese Carnival Pranks," "Fantastic Pieces," and "Scenes from a Childhood," are meant to evoke particular images in the listener's mind. As Donald J. Grout and Claude V. Palisca write in the fourth edition of *A History of Western Music,*

Composer Robert Schumann was a prolific composer of lieder, a musical style based on the literary arts.

Schumann intended his music not only to be considered as patterns of sound, but in some manner to suggest . . . poetic [fantasies]. . . . His music embodies . . . the depths . . . and tensions of the Romantic spirit; it is by turns [passionate] and dreamy, vehement and visionary, whimsical and learned.[68]

Schumann's passionate work reached a pinnacle in 1840 when, his spirits cheered by marriage, the composer wrote 138 lieder in what he called a single "year of song."[69] Some of these titles, "You Are Like a Flower," "Poet's Love," "In the Beautiful Month of May," and "Woman's Life and Love," demonstrate the composer's contented mental state at the time. For the next several years Schumann specialized in specific forms. For instance, in 1841 he wrote only orchestral music, specifically four symphonies; in 1842 it was chamber music that included three string quartets, a piano quartet, and a piano quintet.

Unfortunately the romantic composer's mental health began to imitate romantic literature as he became moody, depressed, and suffered from loss of memory. Like the story of an opera, Schumann began to hear voices in his head, according to Schonberg: "In early 1852, he went through an entire week during which he said that angels were dictating music to him while devils in the form of tigers and hyenas were threatening him with Hell."[70] In February of that year Schumann threw himself into the Rhine River. Although he did not die, his musical voice was silenced as he spent the last few years of his life in a mental institution. He died at the age of forty-six.

Although the composer was dead, his wife, Clara Schumann, who was a virtuoso pianist, continued to play his music. Clara was a child prodigy who had been recognized for her talents at age twelve. After her husband died Clara was given the nickname "Queen of the Piano," as she supported herself

Fanny Mendelssohn in a Man's World

In previous centuries refined young women were forbidden to enter into the "man's world" of composing music. But Fanny Mendelssohn, sister of composer Felix Mendelssohn, was one of the few nineteenth-century women recognized for her musical talents.

Mendelssohn's parents were wealthy and intelligent, and Fanny was provided with the finest education. Both Felix and Fanny showed

Fanny Mendelssohn and her brother Felix.

musical talent and performed public recitals together when they were teenagers. But, according to the website "Fanny Mendelssohn (1805–1847)," she was told by her father at the age of fourteen, "Perhaps music will be his [Felix's] profession, whereas for you it can and must be an ornament, and never the fundamental base-line of your existence."

Denied the right to practice her talents, Fanny married a respectable gentleman and attempted to forget about writing music. She became depressed, however, when she could not compose. When she attempted to publish some of her work, Felix talked her out of it, writing to their mother, "She is far too self-respecting a woman for that; she sees to her house and thinks not of the public."

At the age of forty Fanny finally went against her brother's wishes and published some of her work, which was well received by critics. Unfortunately, she died suddenly two years later. Wracked by guilt, Felix had more of her work published before he died only six months later.

and her eight children by giving recitals throughout Europe. During this time she tirelessly promoted her husband's work and that of her friend Brahms. And, at a time when there were few women composers, she also played her own pieces including concertos, lieder, and other piano music. Because of her efforts, the music of Schumann remains popular today.

Program Music

Robert Schumann based many of his pieces on poems meant to evoke specific feelings in the listener, such as the exhilaration of a fresh spring day in the song "In the Beautiful Month of May." Other romantic composers promoted even more ambitious ideas and wrote texts of words or "programs" to be read by the audience before the music was played. With instructions that detailed the images the composer was attempting to convey, "program music" specifically describes stories, objects, or scenery. The concept was defined by composer Franz Liszt as an introduction "added to a piece of instrumental music . . . to direct [the listener's] attention to the poetical idea . . . of it."[71]

By placing poetic images into song the composer inspired moods and intellectual stimulation in the listener. And while composers have long used instruments for sound effects, such as flutes chirping like birds, or kettle drums rumbling like thunder, in nineteenth-century program music this concept was taken to a new height of sophistication as composers used full orchestras in attempts to imitate real-world sounds.

The Vivid Stories of Berlioz

The composer at the forefront of the program music movement is Hector Berlioz, born near Grenoble, France, in 1803. His father was a well-to-do physician who wanted his son to follow him into his chosen profession. Instead Berlioz turned his back on his family's wealth to study theater and singing while learning to play guitar, flute, and piano. Although he had no technical training and did not show himself to be a child prodigy as Mozart and others had, Berlioz had an extremely active imagination that allowed him to create grand compositions of timeless quality.

However strong his imagination might have been, Berlioz, cut off from his family fortune, struggled for years to prove himself to an indifferent public, all the while suffering through a debilitating bout of unrequited love for an Irish actress named Henrietta Smithson. With his life practically defining a romantic soap opera, Berlioz channeled his emotional distress into a grand epic, the 1830 masterpiece of program music called *Symphonie Fantastique*. Sherman and Seldon describe the symphony as having "high passion and graphic 'musical' descriptions of everything from the beauties of nature to a witches' sabbath, from a glittering ball to the composer's opium-clouded vision of his own execution."[72]

A modern performance of Berlioz's epic work of program music, Symphonie Fantastique.

So that listeners would make no mistake, the composer gave the symphony the subtitle "Episode in the Life of an Artist" and wrote an accompanying program whose words explained the autobiographical meaning of the music. Berlioz explained the need for the written words, saying: "The program should be regarded in the same way as the spoken words of an opera, serving to introduce the musical numbers by describing the situation that evokes the particular mood and expressive character of each."[73] What the program clarifies in black and white, the music ex-presses in a wide range of cleverly written sounds meant to soothe, startle, frighten, and even shock the listener. Flutes imitate bird calls, harps create a peaceful mood, timpani drums echo distant thunder, clarinets shriek like wicked demons, guttural trombones spit out a march to the gallows, and violinists hit their strings with the wooden part of their bows to imitate skeletons rattling their bones.

Berlioz won some respect for his experimental symphony, but he also attracted much harsh criticism for producing what some critics simply considered harsh noise. The composer's emotionally turbulent life continued to inspire music on a grand scale, however. As he became more dedicated to proving his worth as a composer, he began to write pieces for huge orchestras that would be sure to gain the attention of critics. For example, although the average orchestra contained about 60 players at the time, Berlioz hired 150 people to play the *Symphonie Fantastique,* an effort considered outrageous at that time. But even this was not enough for the composer who envisioned the "ideal" orchestra as having 467 musicians accompanied by a chorus of 360 singers. This orchestra would include 30 harps, an equal number of pianos, 242 violins, and a range of unusual percussion instruments unheard of in the nineteenth century.

Berlioz never assembled his fantasy orchestra. While he was revered for his visionary ideas by some—and severely condemned by others—he was the first to propose such ideas that later became accepted features of symphonies and orchestras. Decades ahead of his time, Hector Berlioz was the epitome of romantic experimentation.

Lisztomania

While Berlioz was often criticized for his romantic excesses, Hungarian-born pianist Franz Liszt, born in 1811, was one of the biggest stars of his day. Like other romantic composers, Liszt had a deep affinity for literature. He took this love and blended it with a technical wizardry on the keyboard that few have matched.

Liszt loved to experiment with sounds in his pieces, and he used a dramatic and fiery style basic to his Hungarian temperament to perform his works. He studied the folk music of his native land and popularized the song style known as "rhapsody" that incorporates the improvised melodies, fast-paced rhythms, and sentimental passions of Hungarian Gypsy music. He combined these with a flair for performance that created hysterical adoration known as *Lisztomania*, similar to the attention received by modern rock stars. David Pogue and Scott Speck describe Liszt's playing style in *Classical Music for Dummies*:

The Macabre Life of an Artist

The program that Berlioz wrote to accompany his Symphonie Fantastique *is both beautiful and gruesome. It was written by the composer about hope and despair he experienced as a result of his deep love for the Irish actress Henrietta Smithson. Marion Bauer and Ethel P. Peyser describe the program in* Music Through the Ages.

The five movements are entitled: . . . "Reveries, Passions", a free-form movement . . . in which the lover examines his "weariness of soul" and "volcanic love"; . . . "A Ball", in the form of an elegant French waltz, wherein the lover visualizes his beloved at a brilliant [gala]; . . . "Scene in the Country", a [rustic musical poem] . . . in which the artist broods and wonders about her, as shepherds pipe and thunder rumbles in the distance; . . . "March to the Gallows", in which the lover dreams he has killed his loved one and is condemned to death by guillotine (depicted with extreme realism); . . . "Dream of a Witches' Sabbath", [a] . . . fantasy . . . full of "unearthly sounds, groans, shrieks of laughter, distant cries," carried into satire with a parody . . . interwoven in a complex tonal tapestry.

[While] touring all across Europe to sold-out concert halls . . . [Liszt] turned his . . . performances into rockin' road shows: removing a trademark pair of white gloves with a flourish just before playing, insisting on a backup piano onstage in case he broke strings with his violent crashes on the keyboard, and showing off his memorization skills by dramatically tossing the sheet music over his shoulder before beginning to play. . . .

Of course, his fans went wild. So many people wrote to him asking for a lock of his hair that he had to get a dog—he cut off little pieces of fur whenever necessary. *Lisztomania* . . . was out of control. [74]

In addition to writing sixteen Hungarian rhapsodies, Liszt created symphonic poems to Shakespeare's *Hamlet,* Goethe's *Faust,* and Dante's *Divine Comedy.* He also wrote dozens of solo

The talented pianist Franz Liszt plays for the royal family of Austria. Liszt was wildly popular in Europe.

piano pieces that only the most technically skilled musicians can play.

Romantic Italian Opera

While Liszt's impressive performance was seen by large audiences, nothing in the nineteenth century offered as grand a spectacle as opera, which according to David Pogue and Scott Speck in *Opera for Dummies,* utilized "moveable scenery pieces, smoke machines, and even roof-mounted harness rigs that made actors fly around the stage."[75] These grand productions attracted a Who's Who of society's most powerful men and women showing off the latest fashions and hair styles.

Aside from its social context, nineteenth-century opera was the perfect romantic synthesis of overwrought emotion, majestic scenes of nature, and supernatural freakishness. This so-called "union of the arts" according to Bauer and Peyser combined "music, drama, visual effects, dancing, miming and message . . . as one."[76] And while the musical drama was popular throughout Europe, there were two main schools of opera, the Italian and German-Austrian.

The master of Italian opera was Gioacchino Rossini, born in 1792. Rossini was so prolific that he was able to write thirty-eight operas by the time he was thirty-seven years old, and in 1823 alone, twenty-three of his operas were in production somewhere in Europe. Although the composer barely wrote anything in the last half of his life, his works such as *Otello, Cin-*

The great nineteenth-century operas of Giuseppe Verdi are still revered today.

derella, The Thieving Magpie, William Tell, and *The Barber of Seville*, strongly influenced romantic opera composers for the rest of the century.

The Operas of Verdi

Giuseppe Verdi was born in 1813, a time when Rossini was writing about five operas a year. Although he would not match Rossini's output, Verdi is considered one of the greatest composers of nineteenth-century Italian opera and his work remains extremely popular.

Verdi was the son of a poor tavern-keeper in Parma, Italy, an area ripped by political upheaval, revolution, and war.

Unlike many composers who were born to wealth or hailed from musical families, Verdi was of the peasant class. His musical talents, however, allowed him to marry a woman of wealth and stage his first opera, *Oberto,* in 1839. His second opera, the 1842 *Nabucco,* based on the life of ancient Babylonian king Nebuchadnezzar, made him a star in Italy. While the music may sound less than spectacular to modern ears, when the opera debuted, an unnamed critic wrote that the music was "so new, was so unknown, the style so rapid, so unusual, that everybody was amazed."[77]

Verdi's follow-ups to *Nabucco* spread his fame across Europe. He reached his dynamic peak in 1853, composing both *II Trovatore (The Troubadour)* and *La Traviata (The Lost Lady)* in a single year. Along with his 1851 opera *Rigoletto,* based on a story by Victor Hugo, this trio of Verdi productions was performed repeatedly in the years after they were first written, dominating season after season in the opera houses of Paris, London, Rome, Venice, and elsewhere. In 1871 Verdi wrote the masterpiece *Aïda,* commissioned by the Egyptian government for the opening of the Suez Canal.

Verdi's operatic works of genius remain amazingly popular today. More than a century after his death in 1901 his operas are in continual production, and his music has enriched and inspired the lives of millions of fans.

Wagner's Influential Opera

Verdi was the indisputable king of nineteenth-century Italian opera, but he had an archrival in German composer Richard Wagner, who was also born in 1813.

Wagner, called "the greatest Romanticist of all,"[78] was from Leipzig, Germany, and because of his affinity for composing opera he was considered the German version of Verdi. Like many other romantic composers, Wagner was fascinated by literature as a young man and began writing music to literary themes in his teens. Wagner's first successful opera, the 1842 *Rienzi,* helped the composer land a job as the director of opera in Dresden.

After the success of *Rienzi* Wagner began writing his own librettos, or stories to accompany his operas, something few composers ever attempted. By the end of the 1840s Wagner began working on a colossal cycle of four music dramas known as *Der Ring des Nibelungen (The Ring of the Nibelungs),* which included the now-famous *Das Rheingold (The Rhine Gold), Die Walküre (The Valkyrie), Siegfried,* and *Die Götterdämmerung (The Twilight of the Gods).* This monumental undertaking consumed twenty-two years of Wagner's life. This cycle of operas, which Latham and Sadie call the "greatest achievements of Western culture,"[79] is based on ancient tales of gods, giants, humans, and dwarves called Nibelungs. The symbolism behind the stories, however, was meant to relate to real-world political events such as the industrialization of society and the growth of socialism in Europe.

Wagner influenced nineteenth-century music in several areas: He brought German opera to its peak as Verdi

A majestic performance of Wagner's opera Die Götterdämmerung, *the fourth opera in the composer's* Ring *cycle.*

had done with Italian opera. He also created a new form called music drama, best demonstrated in the 1865 *Tristan und Isolde* that alternates scenes of action with dialogue and a narrative monologue. In addition to his musical works Wagner wrote extensively about nineteenth-century politics and culture, throwing his support behind the 1848 revolution in Germany with fiery words of propaganda. Unfortunately, the composer was extremely anti-Semitic, and his anti-Jewish writings later inspired Adolf Hitler and the Nazis in the twentieth century. Although this has left Wagner despised by some modern critics, his musical drama was unequaled in the romantic era. As Latham and Sadie write:

As no one had done before, [Wagner] changed opera—not just opera, but music itself. Nor just music, but indeed art: the impact of this man, his creations and his thought, left the world a different place. He arouses men's passions, intellectual and emotional, as no artist had done before, nor any since. . . . He has been hailed as a high priest of a thousand philosophies. . . . His music is hated as much as it is worshipped. The only issue beyond dispute is his greatness. [80]

The Experimental Age

As the works of Wagner demonstrate, the romantic era was a time of burgeoning creativity when composers attempted to portray real-life events symbolically through music. By using lieder, tone poems, program symphonies, and other styles, music and literature were brought together as never before.

During an age of wars and revolution romantic composers felt free to make music that was, at times, violent and macabre. In some of the chaotic pieces of Berlioz the music almost borders on madness. Despite the controversies, the works of romantic composers stand as monuments to an age when the untried and experimental was allowed to flourish in a world hungry for the new.

Chapter Six

The Modern Era

In the modern era, from about 1890 to 2001, dedication to pushing musical boundaries took precedence over what the average audience might appreciate or understand. Musical rules established as long ago as the tenth century—concerning harmony, chord progressions, and other foundations of music—were sometimes abandoned as composers attempted to capture the sounds of the modern, industrial world.

In a world drastically changed by the introduction of electricity, automobiles, airplanes, radio, television, recorded music, mechanized warfare, nuclear bombs, and rockets to the moon, it is not surprising that the musical rules of earlier times were upended, scrambled, and—in some cases—rearranged beyond recognition.

New Chords for New Music

In the early years of the modern era, the pounding chords and dissonant harmonies of Igor Stravinsky's *The Rite of Spring* literally caused riots in Paris in 1913 because the crowd felt that Stravinsky's groundbreaking composition was actually a blasphemous effort to destroy music. But dissonance—music written with combinations of notes that sound off-key but are meant to suggest unrelieved tension—would come to be a guiding force among the leading composers of the twentieth century. Stravinsky himself tried to explain the importance of dissonance in composition when paired with its musical opposite, consonance:

Consonance . . . is the combination of several tones into a harmonic unit. Dissonance results from the deranging of this harmony by the addition of tones foreign to it. . . . Ever since it appeared in our vocabulary, the word "dissonance" has carried with it a certain odor of sinfulness . . . [but] in textbook language, dissonance is an element of transition . . . [an] interval of [notes] that is not complete in itself

A contemporary ballet company performs Igor Stravinsky's revolutionary and controversial composition The Rite of Spring.

and that must be resolved to the ear's satisfaction into a perfect consonance.[81]

Although Stravinsky's music was considered controversial at the time, it paled next to the experiments of those who followed, such as the discordant twelve-tone compositions of Arnold Schoenberg or the protracted minutes of silence found in the work of John Cage. These composers were attempting to create atmospheres, sonic spaces, or moods, called ambience, instead of composing songs to which listeners could hum along with the melody. In *The Ambient Century,* rock musician Brian Eno explains this profound shift

in music: "[The] major revolutions in music have been described as changes in the ways composers put notes, chords and instruments together. . . . [And one] very strong movement . . . was towards music as an . . . environmental experience. . . . It's a drift away . . . from performed event to sonic space."[82]

This move towards ambient music was inspired by the late nineteenth-century art movement known as impressionism led by artists such as Claude Monet and Pierre-Auguste Renoir. Instead of painting a scene as realistically as possible, impressionist artists used soft pastel colors to create works with indistinct blurred outlines. This gives the artist's idea, or impression, of a scene, rather than a concrete image. Impressionist paintings appear to be created on the spur of the moment, with bright colors that are unblended with those nearby. Dark tones are avoided, giving the paintings an unusual radiance. Fine details are omitted so that the viewer can receive a general mood or feeling from the work.

Debussy's Artistic Inspiration

The leading composer inspired by impressionism was Claude Debussy, born in 1862. Like impressionist artists, Debussy worked from a palette of bright musical colors that painted vivid musical pictures of peaceful summer days or

Riot Over *The Rite of Spring*

When modernist composer Igor Stravinsky's ballet The Rite of Spring *debuted in Paris on May 28, 1913, the intense, dissonant, rhythmic music and pagan dances depicting ancient Russian fertility rites shocked audiences. The audience responded to the music with whistles and catcalls that grew so loud the dancers could not hear the music. Eyewitnesses describe a society matron slapping a tuxedo-clad gentleman in order to silence his booing. Soon fistfights broke out in the aisles before police arrived to quell the riot. The following excerpt from the composer's 1936 book* Stravinsky: An Autobiography *describes the riot:*

The Sacre du Printemps 'The Rite of Spring' was given on May 28 at the evening performance. . . . As for the actual performance, I am not in a position to judge, as I left the auditorium [to stand in the wings] at the first bars of the prelude, which had at once evoked derisive laughter. I was disgusted. These demonstrations, at first isolated, soon became general, provoking counter-demonstrations and very quickly developing into a terrific uproar. During the whole performance I was at Nijinsky's [the choreographer's] side in the wings. . . . He was standing on a chair, screaming . . . [out the beat] to keep time. Naturally, the poor dancers could hear nothing by reason of the row in the auditorium and the sound of their own dance steps. I had to hold Nijinsky [back], for he was furious, and ready to dash on stage at any moment and create a scandal. Diaghilev [the producer] kept ordering the electricians to turn the lights on or off, hoping in that way to put a stop to the noise.

serene moonlit forests. The titles of his major compositions read like the names of impressionist paintings: *Clouds, Festivals, The Island of Joy, Reflections in the Water, Prelude to an Afternoon of a Faun,* and *The Sea.*

While Debussy had critics who claimed that his music was vague and indefinable, as Mark Prendergast writes in *The Ambient Century,* "[His] strange floating and escaping harmonies and his grasp of instrumental timbre . . . earned him the title 'Father of Modern Music'. Certainly, the high points of the twentieth-century electronic music, like [rock legend] Pink Floyd's *Dark Side of the Moon,* were first envisaged in Debussy's ample imagination."[83]

Debussy himself put it more simply, stating: "I am more and more convinced . . . that music by its very nature, is something that cannot be cast in a traditional and fixed form. It is made up of colors and rhythms."[84]

Gustav Mahler

Like Debussy, Gustav Mahler was born in 1860 and worked during the late nineteenth and early twentieth centuries. But while Debussy was associated with the pleasant sounds of musical impressionism, Mahler led a tortured existence that was heard in his music.

Mahler was known as a famous conductor in his lifetime, leading symphony orchestras in Vienna, Prague, Leipzig, Hamburg, and New York City. But his life was marked by tragedy. As a child, his father abused his mother, and during one particularly violent

Gustav Mahler's tragic life was reflected in his work.

episode young Gustav heard a street musician playing a happy drinking song. Later in life, Mahler came to realize that he associated joyful music with great sorrow. In another incident, Mahler's daughter died of scarlet fever several months after he wrote a series of pieces called *Songs on the Death of Children.* This left the composer wracked with guilt. Pogue and Speck describe how Mahler's personal grief affected his work: "[His] music is full of . . . instruments screaming at the extremes of their range; moments of ethereal beauty, rage and torment, desolation, or triumph."[85]

As a hard-driving perfectionist, Mahler's compositions took him years to finish. For example, his First Symphony in D took more than a decade to complete. But Mahler used this time to write protracted symphonies, some that stretched to more than an hour in length, with up to six movements. His subject matter was deep—his Third Symphony, according to the program, is nothing less than "an ascent through the realms of existence."[86]

To perform his works Mahler needed extremely large orchestras. For instance, his 1907 Eighth Symphony in E flat is called *Symphony of a Thousand* according to Bauer and Peyser, because "it is scored for two large mixed choruses, a boys' chorus, eight soloists, and an orchestra of 120, and lasts more than two hours."[87]

Using a huge orchestra to produce ponderous works was part of the movement toward artistic self-indulgence that many modern composers would follow. So, too, was Mahler's use of several different keys in one symphony. According to Mann, Mahler "took tonal music to limits where it is sometimes impossible to state what key a symphony by him is 'in'. The fourth symphony, for example, begins in G major . . . and ends in E major. . . . an indication . . . that the music travels from one point to another without having a return ticket, so to speak."[88] Mahler also experimented with almost painfully off-key chords, such as the nine-note dissonant shriek at the apex of the first movement in his Tenth Symphony.

Mahler wrote pieces based on his search for the meaning of life, and in doing so transformed traditional concepts of key, harmony, and other musical rules. He explored new avenues of musical experimentation and inspired many composers who followed in the modern era.

The Twelve-Tone Scale

While Mahler made it acceptable to write symphonies in several keys, composer Arnold Schoenberg abandoned musical keys altogether to make music that was called atonal. As a radical departure from traditional music, atonal music has no fixed key and creates dissonant music, often harsh and unfamiliar to the ear.

Born in Vienna in 1874, Schoenberg did not come from a musical family

Innovative composer Arnold Schoenberg deserted musical keys in favor of atonal music.

and, although he played the violin at eight, did not formally study music until he was almost eighteen. Schoenberg began experimenting with music almost as soon as he began composing it at the age of twenty. A symphonic poem he wrote in 1899 was the first work in which a composer had ever used a trombone glissando, that is a rapid slide through a series of consecutive notes.

Schoenberg's works grew increasingly complicated. His *Songs of Gurre,* which he composed between 1901 and 1911, is so intricate, the composer required extralong music to write it down. It calls for a huge orchestra, and as Grout and Palisca write, "Schoenberg outdid even Mahler . . . in size and complexity of the score and Wagner in [the] violence of expression."[89]

For his 1912 piece *Moonstruck Pierrot,* Schoenberg created a new style of music for twenty songs written in what is called in German *sprechstimme,* or "speech voice." This is described by Sherman and Seldon as "a gliding method of vocal performance midway between speech and song, the singer touching a note but not sustaining it. It produces an eerie effect, perfect for the work's graphic portrayal of creeping madness."[90]

Around this time, Schoenberg decided to dispose of tonality and key signatures completely and begin experiments with atonal music. While doing away with keys, the composer still wanted his works to have an organized form, so around 1924, he created serial music, or twelve-tone music based on a series of twelve notes.

In Schoenberg's twelve-tone system there are no fixed keys, but each note in a scale (C, C#, D, D#, E, F, F#, G, G#, A, A#, and B) is equally important. Melodies are replaced by the "tone row," in which each of the twelve notes has to be played once before they can be repeated. That is, once a note is played, the other eleven have to be presented before the original note can be played again. Compositions consist of sets, or series, of these twelve-note rows. A row might be played backwards, forwards, or by turning the sheet music upside down. Although this method sounds simplistic, mathematicians have calculated that there are a possible 479 million combinations for a twelve-tone row.

Known as serial music, or serialism, this jarring dissonant concept was quite controversial and was panned by critics and the general public alike. In fact, Schoenberg was forced to found a private organization, called the Society for Private Performances, so he could play his music and, according to Sherman and Seldon, exclude the "razor-tongued critics and insult-screaming listeners who had made a shamble of so many open concerts."[91]

Schoenberg, who was Jewish, was forced to flee the vicious persecution of Nazi Germany in the 1930s. He eventually took a post teaching at the University of California, Los Angeles, where he lived until his death in 1951. While his music was admired by many composers, the strange-sounding and difficult-to-understand twelve-tone system was intensely disliked by the concert-going public and, therefore, seldom performed. As the composer wrote four years before his death, "I am quite conscious of the fact that a full understanding of my works cannot be expected before some decades. The minds of the musicians, and the audiences, have to mature ere they can comprehend my music. I know this . . . and I know that . . . it is my historic duty to write what my destiny orders me to write."[92]

Alban Berg and Anton von Webern

Despite the fact that most people could not stand to listen to his music, Schoenberg had many musical disciples in the modern era, particularly Alban Berg and Anton von Webern who devoted themselves to the twelve-tone system. The music composed by these men, however, differs from that of their mentor. For example, according to Grout and Palisca, Berg "invested the technique with such a warmth of Romantic feeling that his music is more readily accessible than that of many twelve-tone composers."[93] Berg even used the system to write two expressionistic operas, *Wozzeck* and *Lulu*.

Webern, on the other hand, used Schoenberg's twelve-tone system to create works reminiscent of an earlier era, giving the music an almost classi-

Schoenberg painted this portrait of composer Alban Berg, who poses with it here.

cal sound. His pieces are also short. For example, the movements of his 1913 Five Pieces for the Orchestra, Opus 10, are thirty-six to forty-nine seconds in length, while larger works, such as the 1938 String Quartet, are only nine minutes long.

Schoenberg, Berg, and Webern oversaw the dissolution of a musical system that had been in place for centuries, beginning with Bach in the 1600s. Twelve-tone music, while shunned by the public, was accepted as a valid system by composers by the 1950s.

The Music of the Avant-Garde

Although the general public did not support twelve-tone music, the style was embraced by a group of young composers who gathered in Darmstadt, Germany, after World War II to study the music of Webern and take it to the next level. This group was known as the avant-garde—another term used in visual arts. Musicians, painters, and filmmakers who work in the avant-garde create pieces that are highly original, unconventional, innovative, experimental, and follow few traditional rules or methods.

The gatherings of avant-garde musicians at Darmstadt nurtured the talents of many composers who influenced music in the second half of the twentieth century. Grout and Palisca describe the situation:

Darmstadt was important in that many of the ideas fostered there spread through the world and stimulated experiments on the part of composers everywhere, including eventually the countries of eastern Europe. But every composer worked independently, striking out in new directions, cultivating his own language, his own style, his own special techniques. There was no allegiance to one consistent body of principles, no well-defined "common practice"

as in the eighteenth and nineteenth centuries.[94]

The music that emerged from those who gathered at Darmstadt is known as "total serialism," which lacks tonality, melody, rhythm, and harmony—elements that are contained in almost all other music. In a continuation of Schoenberg's twelve-tone system, other aspects of the music, including the duration of each note, the timbre of the instruments, length of silences, musical texture, and even volume, are played in a repetitive row. Grout and Palisca describe the music that resulted from this complex musical theory:

[Music] based on these principles was . . . *athematic:* that is, it had no themes in the . . . sense of [melody, rhythm, or harmony]. . . . [And there was not] any sense of progression, of movement toward definite . . . points of climax . . . toward the end of the work . . . as had been characteristic of the symphony . . . from the time of Haydn through the nineteenth century. Instead, one was aware only of successive, unrepeated, and unpredictable musical "events." Such events might take the form of . . . "points" of sound—color, melody, rhythm—intertwining, dissolving into one another in an apparently random fashion. Of course, when a work was well constructed . . . [the sound would] form a logical pattern, but it might be a very complex one which only became [audible] after much study and repeated hearings.[95]

New Instruments, New Sounds

The serialism movement influenced composers who were speeding off in every direction to outdo one another in pursuit of the most outrageous avant-garde sound picture. In doing so, they were eager to utilize a new array of electronic musical devices that became available during the 1950s. For instance, French composer Edgard Varèse, who composed for percussion instruments, metal chains, anvils, and sirens in the 1930s, reappeared in 1958 with *Poèm Electronique,* one of the most influential early pieces of electronic music. The work was composed on eleven separate tracks available on a piece of recording tape. Eight minutes in length, *Poèm Electronique* is layered with bells, piano, organ, and various electronically enhanced voices, rhythms, and drums. Repeating tape loops were played at different times over 425 loudspeakers at the Brussels World's Fair, creating not a single song but an ambience, or mood, for the total environment of the fair. The music, heard by over 2 million people, was accompanied by a series of flashing colored lights, possibly the first light show. Prendergast describes the importance of the work:

By demanding twentieth-century instruments for a twentieth-century sound, Varèse was practically applying Debussy's dream of a new music. In his writings Varèse precisely predicted the rise of synthesizers and the role of sampling equipment in creating new sounds. . . . What is striking is that his ideas for light and color projection, his use of . . . the sound environment of *Poèm Electronique* were a blueprint for Ambient Techno Music of the 1990s. [96]

Varèse was joined by a wide array of composers whose interest in electronic instruments was matched by their pursuit of serial, ambient, and experimental music. German composer Karlheinz Stockhausen, an alumnus of the Darmstadt gatherings, was the leading composer of the avant-garde. After playing jazz on oboe, violin, and piano during World War II, Stockhausen practiced "musique concrete," or "concrete music," a style that involved recording various sounds on tape, then cutting and splicing the tape at various angles to produce different attacks and tapering off of sound. This technique often produced a pleasing random kaleidoscopic sound.

In addition to his musique concrete, Stockhausen was a studio wizard who generated a wide variety of sounds using electronic means. When he traveled to the United States to lecture at UCLA in 1966 he met with the Grateful Dead and Jefferson Airplane, who were pioneering the psychedelic San Francisco sound, and greatly influenced their work. He also worked with John

Stockhausen's Space Music

In The Ambient Century *Mark Prendergast describes the music of Karlheinz Stockhausen in the 1970s.*

At the height of his fame Stockhausen would be the star of the World Fair of 1970 held at Osaka. Inside West Germany's spherical metallic-blue pavilion, dotted with points of light, an instrumental ensemble augmented by electronics would perform over a nine month period all of the works Stockhausen had written up to then. For five and a half hours each day the composer would balance and control the sound from a large mixing console via fifty-five loudspeakers arranged in seven rings. A total of one million listeners were attracted to this futuristic scenario, reminiscent of "musical space travel". A visit to Ceylon would produce two ethno-acoustic pieces, *Ceylon* and *Mantra*. . . .

With *Mantra* the idea of "formula music" came into play. This was a technique whereby a simple musical idea could be expanded over time. . . . [Here] Stockhausen was dealing with a piano [pattern] treated by various electronics at a Munich studio. The result was considered to be beautiful and . . . [serene]. More meditative still was *Tierkreis (Zodiac)*, a series of . . . melodies based on the twelve signs of the zodiac. With versions for percussion, chamber orchestra, clarinet and piano, it was to become Stockhausen's most popular work.

In 1977 . . . Stockhausen . . . [devoted] himself to the creation of an enormous opera cycle, *Licht (Light)*, for solo voices, solo instruments, solo dancers, choirs, orchestras, ballet, electronic sound and concrete music. This massive concept, encompassing the history of the [universe] based on the [importance] of the seven days of the week in various cultures, was Stockhausen's attempt to outdo [the long compositions of] Wagner by creating the longest "total-art piece" . . . in the history of music. Each "day" would have its own opera lasting several hours, and each opera would take three and a half years to execute, with various parts staged around Europe.

Avant-garde composer Karlheinz Stockhausen's influence can be heard in several songs by the Beatles.

Lennon of the Beatles, and his musique concrete technique can be heard in the Beatles' songs "Revolution 9," and at the ends of "Strawberry Fields Forever," and "Being for the Benefit of Mr. Kite."

The Sounds of Silence

Stockhausen spent the 1970s performing electronically generated music that sounded like it was from outer space. Meanwhile, American avant-garde composer John Cage, influenced by the Zen Buddhist belief that the highest

purpose is to have no purpose, composed music that was based on natural sounds. The end result of this concept was the 1952 piece "4'33," a work of silence that lasted four minutes, thirty-three seconds in which the ambient sound of the concert hall—people shifting in their seats, coughing, whispering to one another, and so on—was intended to be the evening's music. BBC World Service explains:

Throughout his life . . . Cage was celebrated for his various efforts

A Song Played for 639 Years

John Cage was an avant-garde composer whose most famous work is four minutes and thirty-three seconds of silence. Although he died in 1992, interest in his work remained high, and in 2001 German organizers formed a plan to play Cage's composition "As Slow As Possible," for more than six centuries, as the following September 2001 article from BBC World Service explains.

The world's longest performance of a piece of music is being played in Germany, and it will go on playing for another 639 years.

John Cage's composition ASLSP, or to give it its full title As Slow As Possible, is part of what organisers have described as 'a revolution in slowness'. . . .

Last week, The John Cage Project launched what they claim will be the world's longest musical recital. Organ2/ASLSP is due to be performed on the town organ in Halberstadt in northern Germany over a decidedly leisurely 639 years.

Apparently some 360 spectators, paid [about $15] to see the recital's organist inflate his instrument's bellows and they'll have to come back in another 18 month's time in order to hear him play the first chord—

and one each year or so thereafter.

Providing that sponsors can be found, the performance is scheduled to reach its finale in 2640, with a half time interval planned in 2319.

Although Cage originally wrote ASLSP in 1992 as a 20-minute piece for piano, for many years musicologists have deliberated over just how slow, as slow as possible really is.

Whilst purists have argued that time is infinite, the John Cage Organ Foundation agreed on the figure of 639 years to correspond with the number of years since the construction of Germany's first block single organ.

Eccentric composer John Cage (right) is seen with artist Andy Warhol (center) in 1966.

to subvert audiences' conventional concepts of what music is, and should be. Famously quoted as saying, "if my work is accepted I must move on to the point where it isn't", Cage continually pushed back artistic boundaries and led audiences to the edge of reason.[97]

Bach to Techno

The music of the Western world has changed considerably over the past one hundred years. Chants reminiscent of those played in the thirteenth century are heard on television commercials and fifteenth-century madrigals are regularly played at annual Renaissance Festivals. The musical styles of Bach, Mozart, and Beethoven have been deconstructed, rebuilt, and even blended with jazz, rock and roll, and techno music.

In an era when the ring of a cell phone can play the opening notes of Beethoven's Fifth, the musically impossible has become commonplace. Western music, which once followed strict rules overseen by church and government officials, is now open to experimentation by a new generation of composers raised on the Beatles, Beck, and Snoop Doggy Dog. Where music was once confined to the palace, the church, or the exclusive concert hall, it can now be heard in movie theaters, automobiles, and on CDs and personal computers. While some might wonder if Mozart would approve of what has happened to his beloved music, he would surely approve that the music once heard only by a select few has come to be loved by so many millions of people around the world.

• Notes •

Introduction: When All Music Was Classical

1. Stanley Sadie and Alice Latham, eds., *The Cambridge Music Guide.* Cambridge, UK: Cambridge University Press, 2000, p. 21.
2. Robert Sherman and Philip Seldon, *The Complete Idiot's Guide to Classical Music.* New York: Alpha Books, 1997, p. 6.
3. Sherman and Seldon, *The Complete Idiot's Guide to Classical Music,* p. 6.

Chapter One: Music of Medieval Times

4. William Mann, *James Galway's Music in Time.* New York: Henry N. Abrams, 1982, p. 14.
5. Donald Jay Grout, *A History of Western Music,* rev. ed. New York: W.W. Norton, 1973, pp. 11–12.
6. Dhun H. Sethna, *Classical Music for Everybody.* Sierra Madre, CA: Fitzwilliam, 1997, p. 43.
7. Paul Bekker, *The Story of Music.* New York: W. W. Norton, 1927, pp. 49–50.
8. Grout, *A History of Western Music,* pp. 21–22.
9. Douglas B. Killings, "The Song of Roland," The Online Medieval and Classical Library, 1995. http://sunsite.berkeley.edu.

10. Sadie and Latham, *The Cambridge Music Guide,* p. 90.
11. Grout, *A History of Western Music,* p. 62.
12. Grout, *A History of Western Music,* p. 76.
13. Mann, *James Galway's Music in Time,* pp. 94–95.

Chapter Two: The Musical Renaissance

14. Sethna, *Classical Music for Everybody,* p. 61.
15. Sadie and Latham, *The Cambridge Music Guide,* p. 97.
16. Quoted in Romain Goldron, *Music of the Renaissance.* New York: Doubleday, 1968, p. 9.
17. Quoted in Will Durant, *The Renaissance.* New York: Simon and Schuster, 1953, p. 599.
18. Durant, *The Renaissance,* p. 599.
19. Mann, *James Galway's Music in Time,* p. 37.
20. Quoted in Dom Anselm Hughes and Gerald Abraham, eds., *Ars Nova and the Renaissance 1300–1540.* Oxford: Oxford University Press, 1986, p. 230.
21. Guillaume Dufay, *Dufay Chansons,* trans. Keith Anderson. HNH International, 1996, p. 19.
22. Dufay, *Dufay Chansons,* p. 16.
23. Mann, *James Galway's Music in Time,* p. 39.
24. Mann, *James Galway's Music in Time,* pp. 39–40.

25. Alec Harmon, *Man and His Music Part 1: Mediaeval and Early Renaissance Music.* London: Barrie & Jenkins, 1988, p. 205.
26. Mann, *James Galway's Music in Time,* p. 51.
27. Grout, *A History of Western Music,* p. 234.
28. Quoted in Sadie and Latham, *The Cambridge Music Guide,* p. 135.
29. Durant, *The Renaissance,* p. 605.

Chapter Three: The Baroque Era

30. Quoted in George J. Buelow, ed., *The Late Baroque Era.* Englewood Cliffs, NJ: Prentice-Hall, 1994, p. 1.
31. Quoted in Buelow, *The Late Baroque Era,* p. 1.
32. Quoted in Buelow, *The Late Baroque Era,* p. 1.
33. Sadie and Latham, *The Cambridge Music Guide,* p. 140.
34. Buelow, *The Late Baroque Era,* p. 5.
35. David Ewen, *Opera.* New York: Franklin Watts, 1972, p. 7.
36. Quoted in Ewen, *Opera,* p. 9.
37. Ewen, *Opera,* p. 10.
38. Ewen, *Opera,* p. 13.
39. Sadie and Latham, *The Cambridge Music Guide,* p. 147.
40. Buelow, *The Late Baroque Era,* p. 6.
41. Sherman and Seldon, *The Complete Idiot's Guide to Classical Music,* p. 156.
42. Quoted in Charles Sanford Terry, *Johann Sebastian Bach.* London: Oxford University Press, 1972, p. 70.
43. Albert Schweitzer, *J.S. Bach,* Vol. 1. New York: Dover, 1966, p. 407.
44. Sherman and Seldon, *The Complete Idiot's Guide to Classical Music,* p. 159.
45. Sherman and Seldon, *The Complete Idiot's Guide to Classical Music,* p. 161.

Chapter Four: The Classical Period

46. Sherman and Seldon, *The Complete Idiot's Guide to Classical Music,* p. 155.
47. Sadie and Latham, *The Cambridge Music Guide,* pp. 221–22.
48. Sadie and Latham, *The Cambridge Music Guide,* p. 220.
49. Sherman and Seldon, *The Complete Idiot's Guide to Classical Music,* pp. 76–77.
50. Elaine Schneider, "Franz Joseph Haydn Biography," 2001. http://wawa.essortment.com.
51. Quoted in Neal Zaslaw, ed., *The Classical Era.* Englewood Cliffs, NJ: Prentice-Hall, 1989, p. 268.
52. Mann, *James Galway's Music in Time,* p. 144.
53. Quoted in Sherman and Seldon, *The Complete Idiot's Guide to Classical Music,* p. 170.
54. Quoted in Zaslaw, *The Classical Era,* p. 290.
55. Quoted in Alfred Einstein, *Mozart, His Character and His Work.* New York: Oxford University Press, 1945.
56. Quoted in Hans Gal, ed., *The Musician's World.* New York: Arco, 1965, p. 70.

57. Harold C. Schonberg, *The Lives of the Great Composers.* New York: W.W. Norton, 1981, p. 94.

58. Schonberg, *The Lives of the Great Composers,* p. 109.

59. Sony Music, "Essentials of Music—Composers," 2001. www.essentials ofmusic.com.

60. Quoted in O.G. Sonneck, ed., *Beethoven: Impressions by His Contemporaries.* New York: Dover, 1967, p. 11.

61. Franz Wegeler and Ferdinand Ries, *Beethoven Remembered.* Arlington, VA: Great Oceans Publishers, 1987, p. 88.

62. Mann, *James Galway's Music in Time,* p. 162.

63. Sherman and Seldon, *The Complete Idiot's Guide to Classical Music,* p. 177.

64. Quoted in Alexander Thayer, *The Life of Ludwig van Beethoven,* Vol. 3. Ann Arbor, MI: University Microfilms International, 1989, p. 300.

Chapter Five: The Romantic Era

65. Sherman and Seldon, *The Complete Idiot's Guide to Classical Music,* p. 187.

66. Marion Bauer and Ethel P. Peyser, *Music Through the Ages.* New York: G.P. Putnam's Sons, 1967, p. 405.

67. Bauer and Peyser, *Music Through the Ages,* p. 412.

68. Donald J. Grout and Claude V. Palisca, *A History of Western Music.* 4th ed. New York: W.W. Norton, 1988, p. 686.

69. Quoted in Sherman and Seldon, *The Complete Idiot's Guide to Classical Music,* p. 193.

70. Schonberg, *The Lives of the Great Composers,* p. 181.

71. Quoted in Matt Boynick, "Musical Forms—Program Music," October 10, 2000. http://w3.rz-berlin.mpg. de/cmp/g_programme_music.html.

72. Sherman and Seldon, *The Complete Idiot's Guide to Classical Music,* p. 195.

73. Quoted in Grout and Palisca, *A History of Western Music,* 4th ed., p. 709.

74. David Pogue and Scott Speck, *Classical Music for Dummies.* Chicago: IDG Books Worldwide, 1997, p. 55.

75. David Pogue and Scott Speck, *Opera for Dummies.* Chicago: IDG Books Worldwide, 1997, p. 58.

76. Bauer and Peyser, *Music Through the Ages,* p. 469.

77. Quoted in Schonberg, *The Lives of the Great Composers,* p. 256.

78. Bauer and Peyser, *Music Through the Ages,* p. 493.

79. Sadie and Latham, *The Cambridge Music Guide,* p. 352.

80. Sadie and Latham, *The Cambridge Music Guide,* p. 345.

Chapter Six: The Modern Era

81. Sony Music, "Essentials of Music—Composers."

82. Quoted in Mark Prendergast, *The Ambient Century.* New York: Bloomsbury, 2000, p. xi.

83. Prendergast, *The Ambient Century,* p. 11.

84. Quoted in Sherman and Seldon, *The Complete Idiot's Guide to Classical Music,* p. 212.

85. Pogue and Speck, *Classical Music for Dummies,* p. 60.

86. Quoted in Sadie and Latham, *The Cambridge Music Guide,* p. 394.

87. Bauer and Peyser, *Music Through the Ages,* p. 567.

88. Mann, *James Galway's Music in Time,* p. 300.

89. Grout and Palisca, *A History of Western Music.* 4th ed., p. 849.

90. Sherman and Seldon, *The Complete Idiot's Guide to Classical Music,* p. 217.

91. Sherman and Seldon, *The Complete Idiot's Guide to Classical Music,* p. 218.

92. Quoted in Schonberg, *The Lives of the Great Composers,* p. 602.

93. Grout and Palisca, *A History of Western Music,* 4th ed., p. 859.

94. Grout and Palisca, *A History of Western Music,* 4th ed., p. 865.

95. Grout and Palisca, *A History of Western Music,* 4th ed., p. 866.

96. Prendergast, *The Ambient Century,* p. 36.

97. BBC World Service, "A Time for John Cage: Arts and Entertainment," September 2001. www.bbc.co.uk.

• For Further Reading •

David Buxton and Sue Lyon, eds., *The Great Composers*. Vol. 2. New York: Marshall Cavendish, 1987. One in a series of books written in England about famous composers, their lives, and times. This book about Ludwig van Beethoven also features listener's guides for famous works and many interesting pictures, sidebars, and musical information.

——, *The Great Composers*. Vol. 5. New York: Marshall Cavendish, 1987. Another of the Great Composer series, this one contains biographical, musical, and background notes about Johann Sebastian Bach.

Adèle Geras, *The Random House Book of Opera Stories*. New York: Random House, 1997. The story lines of eight famous operas including Mozart's *The Magic Flute* and Bizet's *Carmen,* accompanied by beautiful illustrations.

Michael Hurd, *Young Person's Guide to Opera*. New York: Roy Publishers, 1968. Information intended to help the novice understand opera with chapters on etiquette, composers, history, and more.

William Mann, *James Galway's Music in Time*. New York: Henry N. Abrams, 1982. The history of Western music in chronological order from the ancient world to the mid-twentieth century with more than 350 paintings, engravings, maps, diagrams, and photographs, and an introduction by renowned flutist James Galway.

Don Nardo, *Mozart*. San Diego, CA: Lucent Books, 1997. Some people believe Mozart was poisoned by his enemies, and this book explores several theories surrounding the composer's death.

David Pogue and Scott Speck, *Classical Music for Dummies*. Chicago: IDG Books Worldwide, 1997. This informative book with the funny name explores the history of classical music, the lives of composers, the workings of symphony orchestras, and other information. The book comes with a very informative CD.

——, *Opera for Dummies*. Chicago: IDG Books Worldwide, 1997. Another in the "Dummies" series, this one exploring every aspect of opera including history, composers, and over fifty story lines to famous operas. Written in an amusing and easy-to-understand format.

Dhun H. Sethna, *Classical Music for Everybody*. Sierra Madre, CA: Fitzwilliam, 1997. A book that explains the complexity of classical music in simple terms.

Robert Sherman and Philip Seldon, *The Complete Idiot's Guide to Classical Music.* New York: Alpha Books, 1997. Despite the silly name, this fun-to-read book is filled with practical facts, interesting sidebars, and useful information, and is extremely helpful to anyone wishing to learn more about classical music.

Roland Vernon, *Introducing Beethoven.* Parsippany, NJ: Silver Burdett Press, 1996. One of a series of books written in England about the influences and historical events that shaped the life of Ludwig van Beethoven. Illustrated in full color with many sidebars about other important cultural events of the time.

————, *Introducing Mozart.* Parsippany, NJ: Silver Burdett Press, 1996. Another book by Vernon, this one detailing the life and times of Wolfgang Amadeus Mozart.

Franz Wegeler and Ferdinand Ries, *Beethoven Remembered.* Arlington, VA: Great Oceans Publishers, 1987. A fascinating and entertaining book—and one of the first biographies—about Ludwig van Beethoven published in 1838. Contains personal memories, original letters, and other interesting information. Wegeler knew the composer from his earliest years and was a close friend his entire life. Ries was a student, protégé, and friend of Beethoven from the time the composer was thirty-one. Originally written in German, this book was not available in English until 1987.

• Works Consulted •

Books

Marion Bauer and Ethel P. Peyser, *Music Through the Ages*. New York: G.P. Putnam's Sons, 1967. First published in 1932, this ambitious undertaking explores the history of music, musicians, and musical styles from ancient times until the twentieth century.

Paul Bekker, *The Story of Music*. New York: W. W. Norton, 1927. An exploration of polyphony, opera, symphony, and other Western music by a German musicologist.

George J. Buelow, ed., *The Late Baroque Era*. Englewood Cliffs, NJ: Prentice-Hall, 1994. A series of essays by leading music experts concerning the era from 1680 to 1740.

Carl Dahlhaus, *Nineteenth-Century Music*. Berkeley: University of California Press, 1989. A scholarly study of music composed and played between the late classical era and the twentieth century.

Hans T. David and Arthur Mendel, eds., *The Bach Reader*. New York: W.W. Norton, 1966. First published in 1945, this book details the life and times of Johann Sebastian Bach in his own words and those of his contemporaries by using source letters and documents gathered together in one volume for the first time.

Guillaume Dufay, *Dufay Chansons*. Trans. Keith Anderson. HNH International, 1996. A booklet accompanying a CD with English translations of Dufay's words originally written in French.

Will Durant, *The Reformation*. New York: Simon and Schuster, 1957. Part 6 of a twenty-book series, "The Story of Civilization," written by a renowned author who, helped by his wife Ariel, spent the better part of his life recording the history of Western civilization.

———, *The Renaissance*. New York: Simon and Schuster, 1953. Part 5 of "The Story of Civilization" by the Pulitzer Prize–winning philosopher, writer, and historian.

Alfred Einstein, *Mozart, His Character and His Work*. New York: Oxford University Press, 1945. A well-written biography of one of the world's greatest composers.

David Ewen, *Opera*. New York: Franklin Watts, 1972. The illustrated story of opera written by a leading musicologist, with details of musical heritage, renowned composers, technical aspects, and story lines.

Hans Gal, ed., *The Musician's World*. New York: Arco, 1965. A book of letters written by and sent to dozens of great composers from Bach to Mozart to Puccini. Also included are letters from composers to other composers and letters written by famous friends and family members of composers.

Romain Goldron, *Music of the Renaissance.* New York: Doubleday, 1968. Volume four of a twenty-one-set series on the history of music written by a renowned Swiss musicologist and art critic.

Donald Jay Grout, *A History of Western Music.* Rev. Ed. New York: W.W. Norton, 1973. The scholarly telling of musical history from the ancient world through the twentieth century.

Donald J. Grout and Claude V. Palisca, *A History of Western Music.* 4th ed. New York: W.W. Norton, 1988. A newer version of Grout's classic work updated by a professor of music at Yale University after the original author died in 1987.

Alec Harmon, *Man and His Music Part 1: Mediaeval and Early Renaissance Music.* London: Barrie & Jenkins, 1988. An insightful reading of thirteenth- through fifteenth-century music that weaves social, cultural, and musical events into a fascinating history.

Dom Anselm Hughes and Gerald Abraham, eds., *Ars Nova and the Renaissance 1300–1540.* Oxford: Oxford University Press, 1986. Part three of the ten-volume New Oxford History of Music series written by leading experts in the field.

W.S.B. Mathews, *A Popular History of Music.* New York: AMS Press, 1974. An examination of music from ancient Egypt to the early twentieth century, first published in 1915.

Yehudi Menuhin and Curtis W. Davis, *The Music of Man.* New York: Methuen, 1979. The story of music from Asia, North America, Europe, and elsewhere.

Mark Prendergast, *The Ambient Century.* New York: Bloomsbury, 2000. A book that covers the shift in the sound of music in the twentieth century where every musical rule was broken or reshaped.

Alan Rich, *Music: Mirror of the Arts.* New York: Frederick A. Praeger, 1969. Dozens of illustrations of classical paintings and a text comparing art with the music of specific eras, such as the Renaissance, baroque, and so on.

Stanley Sadie and Alice Latham, eds., *The Cambridge Music Guide.* Cambridge, UK: Cambridge University Press, 2000. A comprehensive guide to the history, development, and theory of Western music.

Harold C. Schonberg, *The Lives of the Great Composers.* New York: W.W. Norton, 1981. This book details the life of great composers from the Renaissance era to modern times and is written by the senior music critic of the *New York Times,* who was awarded a Pulitzer Prize for criticism in 1971.

Albert Schweitzer, *J.S. Bach.* Vol. 1. New York: Dover, 1966. This volume, first published in 1911, was written by famous humanitarian

Albert Schweitzer, who was also a well-known musicologist. This book is considered one of the classic studies of the composer's life.

O.G. Sonneck, ed., *Beethoven: Impressions by His Contemporaries*. New York: Dover, 1967. First published in 1926, this book records the words written about Ludwig van Beethoven by thirty-nine men who met the genius and were alive at the same time as the composer. Interesting source quotes from those who actually heard the maestro play.

Igor Stravinsky, *Stravinsky: An Autobiography*. New York: Simon, 1936. The life story of the Russian composer whose music inspired the leading composers of the modern era.

Charles Sanford Terry, *Johann Sebastian Bach*. London: Oxford University Press, 1972. First published in 1928, this scholarly work is a formal catalog of the composer's life rather than a critical appreciation of his music. Contains many photos and drawings of places Bach worked and lived and includes a detailed family tree.

Alexander Thayer, *The Life of Ludwig van Beethoven*. Vol. 3. Ann Arbor, MI: University Microfilms International, 1989. The author was one of Beethoven's first biographers who wrote three volumes about the composer in 1866. Thayer began writing only twenty years after Beethoven's death and continued until the author himself died thirty years later. This long detailed biography is the central document upon which many other books about Beethoven have been based.

Neal Zaslaw, ed., *The Classical Era*. Englewood Cliffs, NJ: Prentice-Hall, 1989. Part of the "Man and His Music" series covering the music made in Europe between the 1740s and the end of the eighteenth century.

Internet Sources

BBC World Service, "A Time for John Cage: Arts and Entertainment," September 2001. www.bbc.co.uk.

Matt Boynick, "Musical Forms—Program Music," October 10, 2000. http://w3.rz-berlin.mpg.de.

Rich DiSilvio, "The Franz Liszt Page," Liszt and Modern Music, 2000. www.dvista.com.

"Igor Stravinsky and the 'Sacre du printemps,'" no date. www.music.eku.edu.

Douglas B. Killings, "The Song of Roland," The Online Medieval and Classical Library, 1995. http://sunsite.berkeley.edu.

Erica Land, "MUSL 242: Guillame Dufay (ca. 1400–1474) & the Renaissance," October 10, 1997. www.vanderbilt.edu.

Elaine Schneider, "Franz Joseph Haydn Biography," 2001. http://wawa.essortment.com.

Sony Music, "Essentials of Music—Composers," 2001. www.essentialsofmusic.com.

• Index •

• Picture Credits •

• About the Author •

Stuart A. Kallen is the author of more than 150 nonfiction books for children and young adults. He has written on topics ranging from the theory of relativity to rock-and-roll history to life on the American frontier. In addition, Mr. Kallen has written award-winning children's videos and television scripts. In his spare time he is a singer/songwriter/guitarist in San Diego, California.